Gavin J. Kane

AF239014

Concept and Design of a Hand-held Mobile Robot System for Craniotomy

Concept and Design of a Hand-held Mobile Robot System for Craniotomy

by
Gavin J. Kane

Dissertation, Karlsruher Institut für Technologie (KIT)
Fakultät für Informatik
Tag der mündlichen Prüfung: 16. November 2011
Referenten: Prof. Dr.-Ing. H. Wörn, Prof. Dr. Dr. Georg Eggers

Impressum

Karlsruher Institut für Technologie (KIT)
KIT Scientific Publishing
Straße am Forum 2
D-76131 Karlsruhe
www.ksp.kit.edu

KIT – Universität des Landes Baden-Württemberg und
nationales Forschungszentrum in der Helmholtz-Gemeinschaft

Diese Veröffentlichung ist im Internet unter folgender Creative Commons-Lizenz
publiziert: http://creativecommons.org/licenses/by-nc-nd/3.0/de/

KIT Scientific Publishing 2013
Print on Demand

ISBN 978-3-7315-0018-6

Preface

Some of the work in this thesis has already been published partially as a short paper or as a full contribution in the proceedings of the following conferences: CURAC 2007, Deutsche Gesellschaft für Computer-und Roboter-Assistierte Chirurgie; WC2009, World Congress in Medical Physics and Biomedical Engineering; CARS 2009, Computer Assisted Radiology and Surgery Conference; Human-Computer Interfaces and Measurement Systems; HCI 2009,Human Computer Interface or MICCAI 2008 Medical Image Computing and Computer Assisted Intervention. The work has been mainly done at the Institute for Process Control and Robotics of Karlsruhe, Germany, with the cooperation and the medical supervision of the Oral and Maxillo Facial Surgical Department of the Universities of Heidelberg, Germany. The COMPU-SURGE project is part of the MARIE CURIE ACTIONS, EU-funded Host fellowships for Early Stage Research Training under the Sixth Framework Program.

Karlsruhe,   *Gavin Kane*
November 2011   *Karlsruhe Institute for Technology (KIT)*

i

For Friederike

Abstract

Within the framework of the European Project, *Computer Aided Training for Surgeons and Engineers* (*CompuSurge*) was a solution for minimal impact robotic assisted surgery developed [58] [57].

Problem Background

Craniotomies, surgical procedures involving the opening of the skull, are a common medical option for the correction of a number of medical diseases and problems in Neurosurgery as well as other areas such as Maxillo-Facial Surgery. It can be required as remedy for Intra-cranial bleeding, or to allow surgeons access to intracranial tumours. Additional reasons for performing a craniotomy can include allowing surgeons to insert probes into the brain for treatments of diseases such as Parkinsons, or to assist in the repair of the skull and other cranial problems after trauma. One final reason for performing a Craniotomy is in the treatment of Craniosyntosis. Craniosyntosis, the premature fusion of one or more sutures of the skull, is a rare congenital defect. The standard treatment for a diagnosed case of Craniosynostosis is a surgical remodeling of the skull. In the majority of cases this involves the Fronto-orbital advancement, but can require more complex strategies up to a complete reshaping of the calvaria. The planning for this surgery is based on two significant factors, allowing the brain to grow again normally without any hindrances, and for aesthetic reasons. One significant problem within the surgical procedure is the conveyance of this planning to the patient. The current method involves the surgeon remembering the plan, and using his / her experience drawing fresh the plan on the skull. This method is clearly not accurate, and a second problem is that prior to the craniotomy occurring, this plan can be significantly smudged and distorted. There have been many attempts at performing robot assisted surgeries for this procedure; however, most of them involve the adaption of large industrial robots that impact significantly on the operating room, the surgeon and the surgical workflows. They have been poorly accepted by the surgeons because in this critical section of the procedure, their years of experience are wasted as they only watch.

Aim of the Project

To solve the outlined problems, this work aimed to develop a completely new concept for robotic surgery. A new robot was engineered that was small, mobile and hand-held, capable of seamless integration into the Operating Room with the exact same accuracy of the larger industrial modified robots. In this thesis, I describe the work involved in the system architecture definition, mechatronic design, implementation of the electronic drives, navigation algorithms, software GUI for the surgeon and ancillary safety watchdog systems.

System Architecture and Workflow Integration

The robot was realised as a hand-held mobile robot, with two active driving wheels for navigation along the trajectory. The robot allowed active controlled motion along a trajectory that was pre-operatively planned on a separate workstation. The Surgical Craniotomy Tool is fixed between the two wheels and cuts directly along the trajectory. The position of the robot was tracked passively by an optical tracking system. The surgeon holds and handles the robot like a normal tool, with the speed intuitively controlled through the tilting of the robot.

Mechatronic Design

The first robot prototype was developed and built with two actively driven wheels, and passive control over the cutting depth. This was later further developed to include two more active axes for cutting depth and cutting angle. The robot has a complete weight of only 800gms. The motor section may be removed and after sterilisation reconnected with a self-aligning mechanism. This concept protects the sensitive electronic components and encoders from the heat and moisture during sterilisation. The cutting angle and depth is controlled through a parallel kinematic linkage of the wheel axles. The ability to cut on an angle prevents a disjointed section of bone from being pushed into the cranial cavity and pushing on the brain. To ac hieve the necessary traction on the wheels, an opposing force is generated on the underside of the skull by a hook at the end of the craniotomy tool. The wheels are fitted with spikes which can penetrate the top layer of bone, and maintain grip despite the use of water spray. The wheel design includes a security flange preventing excess penetration and allowing their use on the softer thinner skulls of infants.

Navigation Algorithms and Man-Machine Interfaces

The movement of a mobile robot on a 3 dimensional surface has found very little attention in previous approaches of robot-assisted surgery. In this application, the robot and trajectory segments are tracked in all 6 degrees of freedom. For the navigation of the hand-held robot only three degrees of freedom are required. The use of a Frenet Frame allows this necessary reduction for the control loop without any negative side effects. The tilt of the robot, which is used to control the speed, shifts the cutting axis of the Craniotomy relative to the contact point of the wheels. The same is true for the lateral lean of the robot due to the skull curvature. There variations need to be compensated. This compensation is achieved with adjustment of the Frenet Frame definitions. This Frenet Frame is then used as input to a velocity control loop for the active steering of the robot in minimising the angular error. The robot's velocity is then controlled by the tilt of the robot. The robot tilts around it's wheel axis when the surgeon pushes or pulls intuitively. To determine the inclination, the position upon activation of the drill through its footpedal is used as a reference for each cut.

Safety System Integration

The risk analysis had identified two significant events that could lead to a substantial risk that could not be mitigated within the initial system structure and workflow. The first problem related to a poor registration, and the second was a potential software error. It is very difficult to improve on the registration accuracy of the point to point method used, therefore additional data was collected to allow assessment of the likely validity of the registration. After the point to point registration, the surgeon uses the pointer to trace out the edge of the skin flap on the skull. This data is used for a second registration through the ICP algorithm with the CT data. This registration is not used for navigation, but the correlation between these two registration methods provides an indication to the surgeon on the likelihood of validity. Additionally this data is used as an absolute safety border for the robots navigation. During the operation, further data is then gathered from the robot, updating the ICP algorithm, and maintaining an updated validity check of the registration. The second problem is more serious, that is a software error leads to an interruption in communication, the PID-controlled motors will continue to drive past any safety border at the velocity last set before the communications interruption. To solve this problem, a new Safety Watchdog was implemented on an FPGA to statistically monitor the communications in the system. If any abnormality is detected the motors can be shut off.

Conclusion

This work described a new robot assisted surgical system that could be completely integrated into the surgical workflow that in contrast to previous approaches is highly intuitive to use. The system allows the cutting of accurate craniotomies, based on pre-operative planning and was achieved without the normal drawbacks of robot assisted surgery, specifically without any large influence on the surgical workflow or impact on the layout in the operating room. The system does not attempt to replace the surgeon, but alternately supports them in the critical phase of the operation.

Kurzfassung

Im Rahmen des *Computer Aided Training for Surgeons and Engineers* Projekts (CompuSurge) wurde eine Lösung zur minimal traumatischen robotergestützten Chirurgie entwickelt [58] [57].

Problemstellung

Kraniotomien, chirurgische Eingriffe zur Öffnung des Schädels, werden häufig in der Neurochirurgie sowie in der Mund-Kiefer- und Gesichtschirurgie durchgeführt. Mit dieser Methode können intrakranielle Blutungen behandelt werden und es wird ein Zugang zu intrakraniellen Tumoren ermöglicht. Desweiteren lassen sich mit Hilfe der Kraniotomie Sonden in das Gehirn einführen, um Krankheiten wie Parkinson zu behandeln oder die Reparatur des Schädels und anderer kranialer Probleme nach einem Trauma zu unterstützen. Außerdem kann mit Hilfe der Kraniotomie Kraniosynostose, die vorzeitige Verknöcherung einer oder mehrerer Schädelnähte, behandelt werden.

Die Standardbehandlung für eine diagnostizierte Kraniosynostose ist eine chirurgische Umgestaltung des Schädels, in der Mehrzahl der Fälle durch das "Frontat-orbital Advancement". Außerdem können auch komplexere Maßnahmen bis zu einer kompletten Neugestaltung der Schädeldecke durchgeführt werden. Die Operation hat hauptsächlich zum Ziel, dass das Gehirn wieder normal und ungehindert wachsen kann. Ein zweiter nicht unwesentlicher Faktor ist die Ästhetik.

Die Operation wird vom Chirurg mit Hilfe einer sogenannten Kephalometrie-Analyse basierend auf Röntgenbildern oder CT-Aufnahmen durchgeplant. Ein Problem des chirurgischen Eingriffs ist die Übertragung dieser Planung auf den Schädel des Patienten. In der gegenwärtigen Praxis werden die in die Schädeldecke zu schneidenden Linien von dem Chirurgen per Hand auf den Schädel gezeichnet, wodurch die Präzision des Eingriffs eingeschränkt wird. Ein weiteres Problem ist, dass während der Kraniotomie die Linien verschmieren und verzerrt werden.

Viele Forschergruppen haben daher versucht Kraniotomien robotergestützt durchzuführen. Der konventionelle Ansatz in der robotergestützten Chirurgie ist das Verwenden des Roboters mit einem Fräser, der automatisch von einem Roboter positioniert wird und über eine Kraftregelung die Position des Roboters steuert. Dieser Ansatz erfordert ein komplettes Anpassen des chirurgischen Workflows. Der Arzt hat keine Möglichkeit, das Werkzeug intuitiv zu nutzen. Die erhöhte Genauigkeit kompensiert daher kaum die Nachteile in der Handhabung. Die Akzeptanz bei den Chirurgen ist daher gering, da sie ihre langjährige Kraniotomie-Erfahrung nicht einbringen können.

Zielsetzung

Um die skizzierten Probleme zu lösen, ist das Ziel dieser Arbeit die Entwicklung eines völlig neuen Konzeptes für die robotergestützte Chirurgie. Es wird ein Roboter entwickelt, der klein, mobil und handgeführt ist und nahtlos in den chirurgischen Workflow im OP-Saal integriert werden kann und dennoch eine hohe Genauigkeit erreicht.

In der vorliegenden Dissertation werden die Systemarchitektur, die mechatronische Entwicklung und die Herstellung der Systemkomponenten, die Umsetzung des elektronischen Antriebs für das System, die Unterstützung der Steuerungsalgorithmen und die entsprechende Software mit einer graphischen Oberfläche für den Chirurgen sowie die Sicherheitssysteme beschrieben.

Systemarchitektur und Workflow-Integration

Die notwendige mobile Handführung des Roboters wird durch zwei versetzte Führungsräder realisiert. Sie ermöglicht dem Chirurgen ein aktives Führen auf der an einer Workstation präoperativ geplanten Trajektorie. Hierbei wird die Position des Roboters durch ein passives Trackingsystem erfasst. Der Chirurg steuert lediglich die Geschwindigkeit mit der der Vorgang ausgeführt wird über die Neigung des Roboters. Das chirurgische Kraniotom ist zwischen den beiden Rädern fixiert und schneidet direkt entlang der Trajektorie.

Mechatronische Design

Der erste Roboterprototyp wurde mit zwei aktiven Antrieben und einer passiven Schnitttiefenregelung entwickelt und gebaut. Dieser wurde später mit zwei weiteren Antrieben zur Regelung der Schnitttiefen und –winkelregelung erweitert. Er weist ein Gesamtgewicht von nur 800 g auf. Der Motorenteil kann abgenommen und nach Sterilisation des Hauptteils durch einen sich selbst ausrichtenden Mechanismus wieder mit diesem verbunden werden. Dies schützt die empfindliche Motorelektronik und die Encoder.

Die Winkel- und Tiefenkontrolle für das Schneidewerkzeug werden durch eine Parallelkinematik für die Radachse ermöglicht, die in der Lage ist, unter einem definierten Winkel zu schneiden. Hierdurch wird verhindert, dass ein durch den Fräsvorgang entstandenes Bruchstück des Knochens, in das Schädelinnere fällt und auf das Gehirn drückt. Um die notwendige Traktion der Räder zu erreichen, wird eine Gegenkraft auf der Unterseite des Schädels durch einen Haken am Kraniotom erzeugt. Die Räder sind mit Spikes ausgestattet, die die oberste Schicht des Knochens durchdringen können und trotz des Einsatzes von Wasserspray noch genügend Haftung aufweisen. Sie sind so ausgelegt, dass sie auch für den Einsatz auf dünneren Schädeln von Neugeborenen mit kleineren Schädeloffnungen geeignet sind.

Navigationsalgorithmen und Mensch-Roboter-Interaktion

Die Bewegung eines mobilen Roboters auf einer 3-dimensionalen Oberfläche fand in den bisherigen Ansätzen der robotergestützten Chirurgie noch wenig Aufmerksamkeit. Durch das optische Tracking sind die Roboterpositionen und Orientierungen sowie die Trajektoriensegmente mit 6 Freiheitsgraden definiert.

Für die Navigation des handgeführten Roboters werden aber lediglich 3 Freiheitsgrade benötigt. Der Ansatz über Frenetsche Formeln ermöglicht die Reduzierung der Freiheitsgrade auf die für den Kontrollalgorithmus notwendigen 3 Freiheitsgrade. Durch die Neigung des Roboters, die für die Kontrolle der Geschwindigkeit verwendet wird, wird die Schneideachse des Kraniotoms zu den Kontaktpunkten zwischen Rädern und Schädel verschoben. Das Gleiche gilt für die seitliche Neigung des Roboters und die Höhe der Achse auf Grund der Schädelkrümmung. Diese Abweichungen müssen kompensiert werden. Die Kompensation wird durch eine Anpassung der Frenetschen Formeln erreicht. Gleichzeitig wird der Winkelfehler und -abstand zur Trajektorie des Roboters durch eine geschwindigkeitsbasierte Regelung minimiert. Diese Regelung wird durch die Neigung des Roboters gesteuert und durch das optische Trackingsystem beim Schieben oder Ziehen über die Radachse erkannt.

Die Geschwindigkeit des Bohrers wird über das Fußpedal gesteuert. Für die Bestimmung der Neigung wird die Position des Roboters beim Aktivieren des Bohrers als Referenz verwendet. Dies ermöglicht eine einfache Neuausrichtung des Systems.

Sicherheitssystem

In der Risikoanalyse werden zwei Probleme identifiziert, die möglicherweise zu einer erheblichen Gefahr werden können, da es nicht möglich ist, diese in dem Entwurf des Systemaufbaus zu entschärfen. Das erste Problem betrifft eine ungenaue Registrierung und das zweite potentielle Fehler in der Software. Die Registrierung kann auf Grund von Messungenauigkeiten kaum verbessert werden. Um dennoch die Bewertung der Situation zu erlauben, werden zusätzliche Daten von der Schädeloberfläche aufgenommen. Diese werden für eine zweite Registrierung mittels des ICP mit den CT-Daten verwendet. Diese Registrierung wird nicht für die Navigation verwendet. Besteht eine hohe Korrelation zwischen den beiden Registrierungen, ist die Wahrscheinlichkeit sehr hoch, dass die Registrierung richtig durchgeführt wurde. Die Daten werden vom Chirurgen dadurch aufgenommen, dass er einen Pointer am Rand des Hautlappens bewegt. Dies ermöglicht es, eine absolute Sicherheitsgrenze für die Steuerung zu definieren. Weitere Daten werden zur Laufzeit durch den Roboter aufgenommen. Dadurch erhält man kontinuierlich aktuelle Daten um diese Validierungsmöglichkeit aktuell zu halten.

Das zweite Problem ist in der Bewertung gravierender. Kommt es zu einem Softwarefehler und damit einhergehend zu einer Unterbrechung der Kommunikation, laufen die PID-geregelten Motoren mit der vorher gesetzten Geschwindigkeit weiter. Um dieses Problem zu lösen wird ein separater FPGA verwendet. Dieser erkennt einen Kommunikationsabbruch durch eine statistiche Analyse der eingehenden Nachrichten. Werden Abweichungen festgestellt, werden die Motoren deaktiviert.

Fazit

Diese Arbeit beschreibt ein in den Operationsablauf vollständig integriertes System für die roboterassistierte Chirurgie, das im Gegensatz zu bisherigen Ansätzen intuitiv bedienbar ist. Das System ist in der Lage, genaue Kraniotomien durchzuführen, basierend auf einer detaillierten präoperativen Planung. Dies wird erreicht ohne die üblichen Nachteile der roboterassistierten Chirurgie, insbesondere einen zu großer Einfluss auf den Workflow oder Auswirkungen auf die Anordnung der Geräte in einem Operations-saal. Das System ersetzt den Chirurg nicht, sondern assistiert diesem in einer kritischen Phase der Operation.

Acknowledgement

This work wouldn't have been possible without the help of many people. First of all I would like to thank my supervisor Prof. H. Wörn for his guidance and insight during all my time spent at the IPR, Institute for Process Control and Robotics. I also thank my co-supervisor Prof. G. Eggers for his patience, valuable input and constant medical supervision during my frequent visits in the operation room at the University Clinics of Heidelberg.

I would also like to thank all the group members of MeGI, for the great atmosphere shared during my stay, the warm welcome as a whole to Germany, and of course for putting up with me as I slowly learnt German. Of course special thanks as well to Markus Mehrwald and Willi August, their freindship throughout my time in the IPR was greatly appreciated, and I know it will last for a long time after we all depart in our own directions.

A special thank to the members of the COMPU-SURGE project: Vitor Vieira, Alessandro De Mauro, Matteo Ciucci, Horia Ionescu and Slávik Rastislav: discussions with them have been always stimulating and fruitful. Another thank to the additional medical supervisors, Prof. Dr. R. Marmulla and Dr. R. Seeberger for their valuable inputs during our regular project meetings; thanks to Dr. R. Bösecke for his impeccable financial management and valuable suggestions. I'm grateful for the support the Klinik und Poliklinik für Mund-, Kiefer- und Gesichtschirurgie of the University of Heidelberg gave me.

Many thanks also to the whole IPR group who warmly welcomed me since the very beginning.

A warm hug to all my family who gave me so much support from back home in Australia. A warm thanks as well to the family of my wife Friederike, who have always made me feel welcome, with a home away from home.

Last but not least, a very special thank goes to my wife Friederike, who assisted and helped me during these years with her patience, devotion and love.

Karlsruhe, Novemeber 2011 *Gavin Kane*

Contents

1. Motivation

1.1. The Craniostar Project

The basic concept of the *Craniostar* Project is to develop a complete surgical system that is capable of supporting a surgeon to perform high precision craniotomy operations. Although in comparison to previous robotic systems, the project is intended to provide significant advantages in terms of reduced size, impact, complexity and risk but with increased usability for the surgeon. The engineering goal for the system was recorded as follows:

> *"Develop for integration into a Surgical Environment an intuitively controlled milling machine for Craniotomies"*

1.2. System Setup

The system setup consists of:

- a custom hand-held robot with up to 4 driven degrees of freedom built around a standard Surgical Craniotomy Drill,

- an optical tracking system, *"Polaris"* (from NDI Inc., Canada),

- a control system inclusive of PC with GUI,

- a security watchdog system, and

- the High Speed Craniotomy Drill Controller for integration.

The control system consists of a computer running both planning software and the robot controller software. The robot controller software conducts all trajectory maneuvre calculations, as well as controlling and maintaining all interfaces with external components including the optical tracking system, the Proportion-Integral-Derivative (PID) controllers for maintaining the wheel velocities, that of the High Speed Drill Controller, and it's foot pedal input. The computer also includes a Graphical User Interface (GUI), which is used by the surgeon to understand the robot's intended movements, and provide a fast overview of the system status. Between the system components are various communication links. This includes an RS-232 link to the optical tracking system, a CAN bus between all the motor controllers and pedal sensors, and a USB link to the Drill Controller interface.

A single watchdog system is used to increase the safety of the system by maintaining an overview of the entire system's functionality, through the monitoring of the system's outputs.

Although both the planning software and the robot controller software are integral to the workflow of the system,, the development in this work concerns only the controller-software, its hardware, and the robot itself. The reader interested in further details related to the planning software is encouraged to read [105].

1.3. Human-robot Interaction

One important goal of the system is integration into the operating room (OR). Therefore a design decision was made early in the project to develop more of an *"Intelligent Tool"* as opposed to a robotic system, this concept was key in the design for a *"hand's on"* approach. This decision drove a number of constraints in the device's construction, for example it's shape, size and simplicity for control. The exact nature and evolution of the design to the hand-held mobile robot is explained later in Chapter 4.

The device developed here uses the 6-DOF optical tracking, combined with the underactuated degrees of freedom in the robot, notably the tilt, to understand the surgeons intent. Similar to that of the Segway©, the surgeon pushes the robot instinctively forward, the robot tilts forward around it's wheel axle, the tilt is identified, and the computer controller identifies this as a *"Speed Up"* command. A second intuitive control is added through integration of the Aesculup©High Speed Drill Controller. The surgeon is already comfortable in control of the High Speed Drill Controller through the use of the foot pedal. To maintain the simplicity of design in this system, no additional foot pedals or control buttons are added. Alternately an interface to this pedal provides an input to the control system providing another indication of the surgeons intent. Use of the drill, (i.e. pressing of the foot pedal) provides indication that the surgeon wishes to proceed with the cutting. This input is used as a signal for when the control system should be working at all.

1.4. Medical Motivation

Craniotomies, surgical procedures involving the opening of the skull, are a common medical option for the correction of a number of medical diseases and problems in Neurosurgery as well as other areas such as Maxillo-Facial Surgery. It can be required as remedy for Intra-cranial bleeding, or to allow surgeons access to intracranial tumours. Additional reasons for performing a craniotomy can include allowing surgeons to insert probes into the brain for treatments of diseases such as Parkinsons, or to assist in the repair of the skull and other cranial problems after trauma. One final reason for performing a Craniotomy is in the treatment of Craniosyntosis. Craniosyntosis, the premature fusion of 1 or more sutures of the skull, is a common congenital defect. The standard treatment for a diagnosed case of Craniosynostosis is a surgical remodeling of the skull. In the majority of cases this involves the Fronto-orbital advancement, but can require more complex strategies up to a complete reshaping of the calvaria. The planning for this surgery is based on two significant factors, allowing the brain to grow again normally without any hindrances, and for aesthetic reasons. One significant problem within the surgical procedure is the conveyance of this planning to the patient. The current method involves the surgeon remembering the plan, and using his / her experience drawing fresh the plan on the skull. This method is clearly not accurate, and a second problem is that prior to the craniotomy occurring, this plan can be significantly smudged and distorted. There have been many attempts at performing robot assisted surgeries for this procedure; however, most of them involve the adaption of large industrial robots that impact significantly on the operating room, the surgeon and the surgical workflows. They have been poorly accepted by the surgeons because in this critical section of the procedure, their years of experience are wasted as they only watch. The following chapter expands on this motivation.

2. Scientific Grounding

2.1. Medical Grounding

2.1.1. Medical Reasons for requiring an opening of the skull

The opening of the skull is termed a Craniotomy, and is a common surgical procedure in Neurosurgery as well as other areas such as Maxillo-Facial Surgery. It can be required as remedy for Intra-cranial bleeding, or to allow surgeons access to intracranial tumours. Additional reasons for performing a craniotomy can include allowing surgeons to insert probes into the brain for treatments of diseases such as Parkinsons, or to assist in the repair of the skull and other cranial problems after trauma. One final reason for performing a Craniotomy is in the treatment of Craniosynostosis.

2.1.2. Craniosynostosis

Craniosynostosis, the premature fusion of 1 or more sutures of the skull, is a rare congenital defect.

The condition may be of prenatal or perinatal onset and, in rare cases, can occur later during infancy or childhood. The earlier the premature fusion occurs, the more dramatic the effect on cranial growth and development. Genetic and environmental factors are involved in the etiopathogeneses of these diseases, and more than 150 syndromes with this developmental defect have been characterized ([20],[8],[111]).

The occurrence of Craniosynostosis according to literature varies considerably, but can be considered to occur between approximately 1 in 2100 births (see [67] and [68]) to 1 in 2500 births [111]. Because of the possibilities of genetic cause of the disease this rate can raise considerably in communities where a higher rate of inbreeding occurs. The rate of occurance is often calculated on the number of births, and the number of reported cases for surgery over a certain time frame; therefore the actual rate of occurrence may be considerably higher, as many of the milder cases are likely to go without surgical treatment. However, even with this consideration, like Lajeunie's assessment, it is difficult to accept the rates offered by Gordan [45], who noted the occurrence to be as high as 1 in 100 for Africa children.

There are many different types of Craniosynostosis, depending on which suture and to what degree and how early the sutures fixate. However, for the purposes of surgical therapy, only 5 skull forms are distinguished[75]:

- trigonocephaly

- plagiocephaly

- oxycephaly

- brachyocephaly

- scaphocephaly

Additionally combinations of these forms are possible according to the sutures affected[130].

The results can lead to very different shapes of the skull. Some examples are shown in Figure 2.1.

Untreated progressive craniosynostosis leads to inhibition of brain growth and increased intracranial and intraorbital pressure. The impending result manifests in neurological symptoms such as headaches, restlessness, sleeping disorders, frequent crying, vomiting, feeding difficulties and failure to develop.

Because of the frequent occurrence of craniosynostosis and the availability of time and data for planning the surgical treatment, the Craniosynostosis is targeted as the main use for the robot developed throughout this thesis.

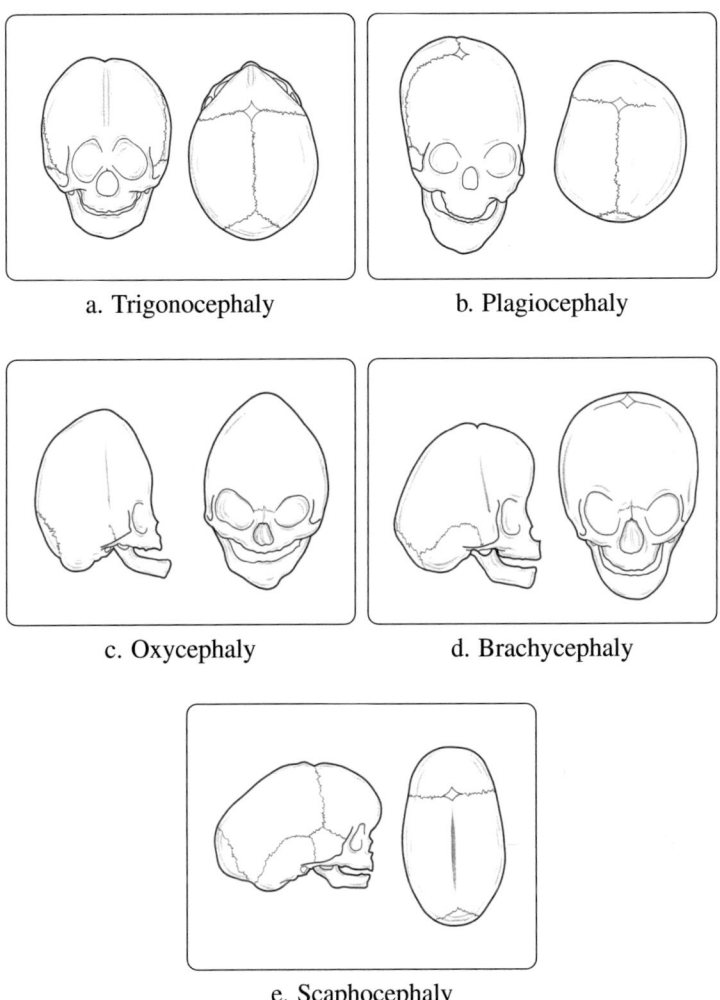

a. Trigonocephaly

b. Plagiocephaly

c. Oxycephaly

d. Brachycephaly

e. Scaphocephaly

Figure 2.1.: Example types of Craniosynostosis.

2.1.3. Diagnosis of Craniosynostosis

Identification of craniosynostosis using a physical examination has been well described in the literature ([54],[56],[112]), and can be confirmed if necessary using a plain skull X-ray or CT scan. CT scans are not thought to be needed for the majority of children, and thus concerns about the unnecessary adverse effects of radiation can be avoided with careful clinical examination ([36]).

2.1.4. Treatment for Craniosynostosis

The standard treatment for a diagnosed case of Craniosynostosis is a surgical remodeling of the skull. In the majority of cases this involves the Fronto-orbital advancement[86], but can require more complex strategies including:

- Fronto-orbital advancement with linear craniectomy,

- Fronto-orbital advancement with total craniectomy,

- Fronto-orbital advancement with Le Fort III Osteotomy,

- occipital advancement, or

- complete reshaping of the calvaria.

The standard technique of the Fronto-orbital advancement is based on the tongue-in-groove technique by Tessier and on the early bilateral advancement introduced by Machac[130]. This technique is based on the osteotomy, removal, modeling and displacing of the frontal-orbital region. Osteotomy lines are placed along the cranial sutures and reaching as far as the cranial base thus eliminating the restrictive influence. The intracranial volume can be increased by repositioning the bone segments. By individually shaping and repositioning the fronto-orbital bone segments, the deformity can be corrected and further development of the skull can be guided in a more favourable direction.

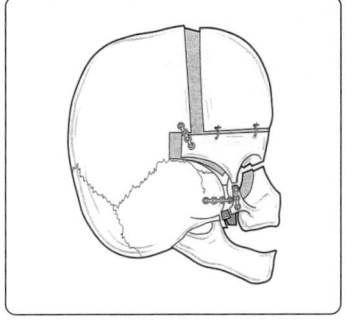 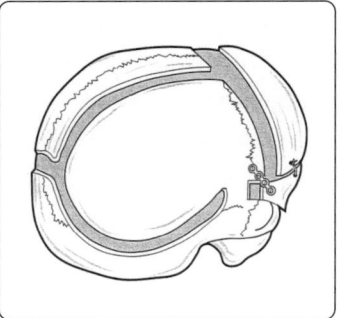

a. Fronto-orbito-maxillary advancement

b. Fronto-orbital advancement with a linear craniectomy

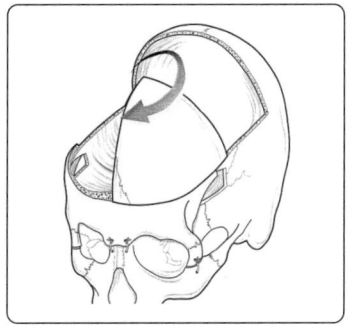

c. Reshaping the calvaria

Figure 2.2.: Conceptual views of surgical options in treatment of craniosynostosis, from [130]

2.1.5. The workflow of the Craniotomy Procedure

A complete surgical treatment can take over 2 hours from first incision to closure of the skull, and over 3 hours when anaesthesia times are included. The complete workflow for a surgery involves approximately 18 steps, and an example is provided in appendix 1. The exact workflow for achieving this, varies from hospital to hospital and often from doctor to doctor. However, for the purpose of this thesis, the workflow steps shown in this appendix will be used for reference.

For example, some different procedures can include the replacement of the craniotomy drill piece with an ultrasonic cutter ([28]). This removes the requirement for the placement of the bore holes, but can double the timeframe of the surgery ([43]) due to the slow speed of cutting with the piezoelectric device. Thus overall the change in the workflow is only minor and not further discussed here.

2.1.6. Planning of Craniosynostosis Treatment Surgery

Two significant goals of the craniotomy, when used as part of the treatment of craniosynostosis, is firstly to increase the intracranial volume allowing the brain to grow normally; and secondly for aesthetic reasons. This aesthetic goal, is for both the parents hoping to have a normal looking child, and also for the child to be accepted normally as they grow up.

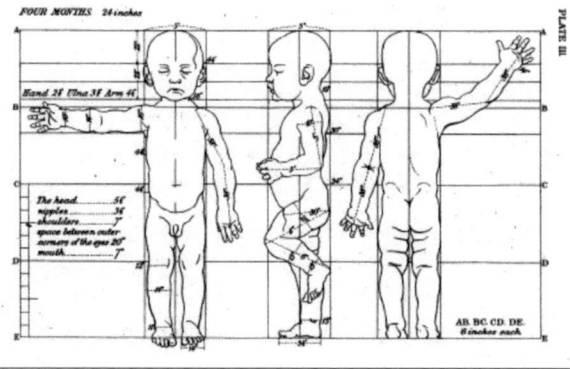

Figure 2.3.: Example of acceptable proportions of human growth shown from [116]

It has been long accepted that there are 'acceptable' proportions of a human body. As medicine has been developed in the last century, these proportions have been formalised, see Figure 2.3. These proportions have been further formalised for the cranial region and can thus be used to plan exactly how far different sections of the skull need to be moved during a surgery bringing the cranial shapes back into proportion and symmetry. Figure 2.4 shows some of these measurements that can be made for the skull. The relation between the measurements then determines the appropriate proportions. For example, Figure 2.5 and 2.6 shows one example classification.

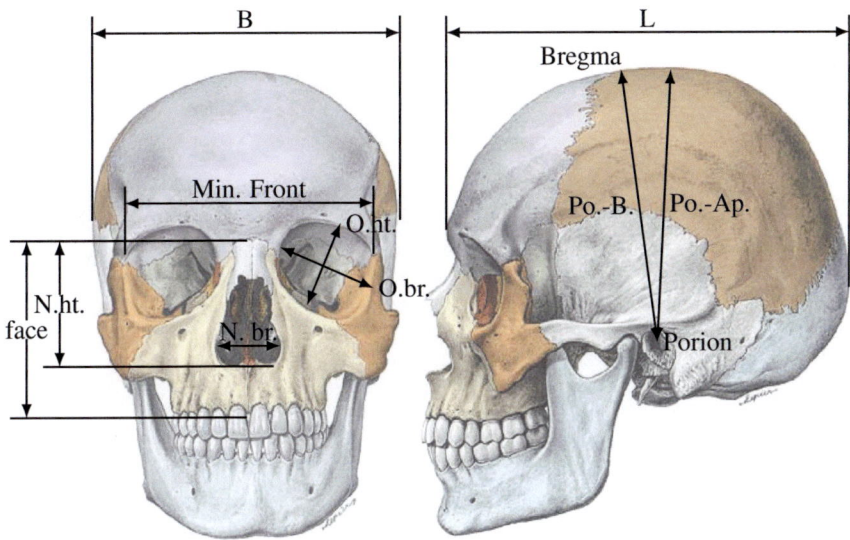

Figure 2.4.: Example skull measurements for Cephalic Analysis. (Images enhanced from Atlas provided by Roche)

To determine these measurements, and the coexisting discrepancies, a surgeon can use a combination of physical measurements of the child together with measurements made from tracings of pre-operative images such as X-Rays, or use modern commercial imaging packages using three dimensional CT or MRI data. These measurements are compared against 'norms' to determine the degree of error, and how much change is needed.

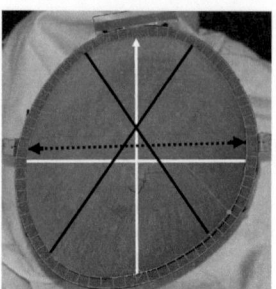

Figure 2.5.: The centre of the nose is indicated by white arrow at top of picture; ear positions are indicated by black arrows at each side. White lines indicate head length and maximum width, dotted black line is ear alignment indicator and black lines indicate oblique cranial lengths. In this example, OCLR = 115.0 and CI = 96.0. From study by Hutchison et al.[55]

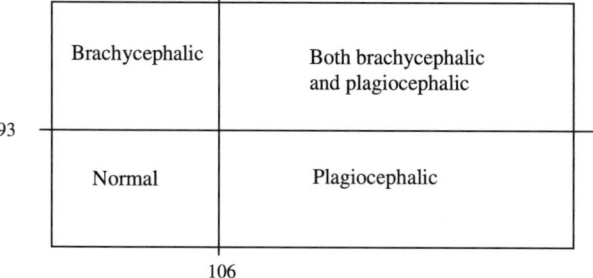

Figure 2.6.: Example usage of skull measurements (OCLR - Oblique Cranial Length Ratio and CI - Cephalic Index) to determine classification of head skull shape, from study by Hutchison et al.[55]

2.2. Computer Aided Surgery and the Craniotomy

There are a growing number of surgical craniotomy procedures in which a precise pre-surgical plan needs to be accurately transferred to the Operating Room (OR). Examples of such procedures include:

- Minimally invasive neurosurgical procedures, where a desired entry hole is pre-planned in order to gain access to a known location of a tumour or other subcranial feature;

- Frontal Orbital Advancement procedures for maxillo-facial surgery, where the desired cranium advancement is pre-planned in order to aesthetically align known facial features;

- Plastic Surgery requiring the milling of bone surfaces according to a three dimensional operation plan [51]; or

- Preparing the skull for CAD/CAM prefabricated skull implants, with the desired skull implant intersection requiring accurate bone resection for better recovery after placement [126].

In support of this requirement for accurate transfer, many research groups have developed robotic solutions specifically to address the challenges associated with the conduct of a craniotomy procedure [126], [32], [7]. To date, none of the solutions have been accepted for commercial clinical use. This has been assessed to be due primarily to three facts:

1. The surgical robotic systems presented are modified industrial robots whose impact within the OR in terms of real-estate and the required changes to surgical workflows and procedures is quite considerable.

2. The risks inherent with the use of a 6-DOF robot performing craniotomies are considerably large, with respect to cutting too deep, causing meninges tears, and possibly thereafter the brain.

3. The robotic solutions offered are all supervisory controlled interventions, which by the definition of Nathoo et al [89] is where the robot performs the pre-planned and programmed movements autonomously, thus removing the surgeon from the procedure. This occurring at the key time when his / her years of experience and 'feel' for the operation are most relevant.

2.2.1. Tracking Systems and Computer Aided Surgical Navigation

One of the most important issues in Computer Aided Surgery is the ability to correlate the virtual world with the real world. In times before the computer aided surgery, this was still a requirement to orientate anatomical structures with atlas based concepts of the body and was first achieved with craniometry. This is the technique of physically measuring the bones of the skull, and defining ones position in a relative manner. It was developed in the 19th century and it is considered the first practical method of surgical navigation. The first tool to achieve this was the stereotactic frame developed by Horsley and Clark in 1908. This is still one of the most precise methods for achieving accurate targeting in surgery today. Modern developments of this system involve the adaption of additional tools directly to the frame for the insertion of needles or probes. This concept for tool tracking has led to the development of a number of different tracking concepts. Optical and Electromagnetic tracking are today prevalent in computer assisted surgery. Mechanical tracking is accepted to be more accurate, but is generally more cumbersome and is not preferred by the surgeons.

2.2.2. Optical Tracking

Optical tracking technologies use a minimum of two video cameras to look at a known configuration marker set. With the two or more cameras can the relative position and orientation of the marker set be determined. A common approach is to use a series of infrared (IR) reflecting marker balls for the marker set. The cameras can then include IR illuminating lamps, achieving a high reflectivity from the marker balls, helping to remove noise from the image, and improving the stability of the position reporting of the system. Alternately the so called passive reflecting markers can be replaced with IR LEDs making the markers active. This can have additional benefits for using the system in areas of high reflectivity, where the LEDs can be syncronised to the cameras, and identified easier.

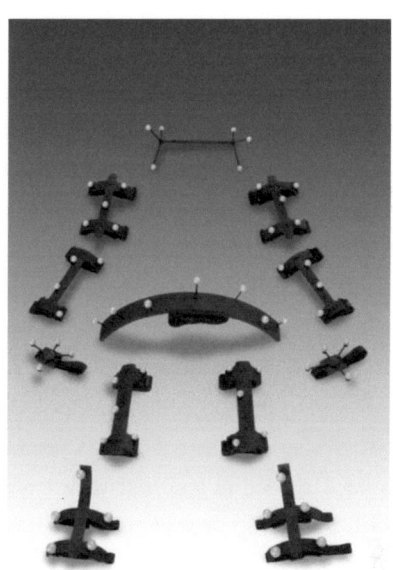

Figure 2.7.: Passive Marker set mounted on an example tool, here a drill / biopsy needle guide

Figure 2.8.: Example marker configurations

In both systems, the accuracy of the tracking is dependent on the configuration of the markers, and the camera distances and separation angles. In many commercial systems such as the Polaris from NDI™or the Vector Vision from Brainlab™the camera separation is set, and a pre-defined volume is constrained within the systems software. The only way for improving the end use accuracy is through the fiducial marker configuration. The analysis of the accuracy related to marker configuration is largely referenced to work by Fitzpatrick [39]. In his key work he demonstrated using perturbation theory that there is a statistical relationship among the expected value of target registration error (TRE), Fiducial Localisation Error (FLE), the number of fiducials (N) and the spatial distribution of the fiducials. The key equation according to Fitzpatrick is shown as 2.1.

$$\langle TRE^2(r) \rangle = \frac{\langle FLE^2 \rangle}{N} \left(1 + \frac{1}{3} \sum_{k=1}^{3} \frac{d_k^2}{f_k^2} \right) \tag{2.1}$$

Where d_k is the distance of the target point r from the kth principal axis of the fiducial point set, and f_k is the rms distance of the fiducials from the kth axis (f_k is effectively the radius of gyration of the fiducial set about its kth principal axis). The key outcome of this equation was a practical evaluation between an overall fiducial set size and its inherent accuracy. The larger the set size, the more accurate a combination could be, for a target point closer to the centre of the fiducial set. However, clearly the larger the fiducial set, and the closer the fiducial set is to the desired target, the greater the hindrance to the surgeon in his/her work. The practical outcome here, was what is now seen as a standard practice whereby marker sets with 3 - 6 markers, spaced in a cluster with a maximum spread of 5 - 10cm, with a length to tool tip of < 20cm is acceptable, for achieving accuracies, after registration (discussed in section 2.2.6), of less than 2mm for the majority of a target organ.

2.2.3. Electromagnetic Tracking

In electromagnetic tracking, sensor coils are embedded in the tools that are being tracked. A field generator is then used to generate and emit electromagnetic waves into the target area. When the tools are placed into the field, currents are induced in the coils that can be used to generate voltages on external measuring ICs. A single coil can be used to generate position and orientation data to 5 DOF, but two coils are required for complete fixation of a tool.

Since the fields are magnetic and of low power, they are harmless for living tissue, and tracking can be conducted without line of sight, even inside a body. This is strongly in contrast to optical tracking. However, this tracking method has not had complete acceptance to the Operating Room due to the interference other metallic instruments can have on the accuracy of the system. They do still hold potential for greater accuracy, because the coils can be produced so small that they can be inside the tip of a surgical instrument. Thereby removing any scaling of the positioning error due to a rotational error.

2.2.4. Mechanical Tracking

Mechanical tracking is known to be the most accurate of all possible tracking systems. Noises are reduced by development of larger more rigid structures. However, the requirement for the tools to be physically attached to a serial kinematic mechanism to the ground, roof or operating table is also the greatest hindrance to their use, and hence acceptance as effective tools inside the operating room.

2.2.5. Patient Tracking

With any of the above methods (or combination thereof) several transformation matrices must be computed to enable the tracking of an intra-operative tool in a coordinate space relative to the patients image, see Figure 2.9. $M_T L$ represents the position and orientation of the tracked probe inside the coordinate system of the camera. $M_W T$ represents the position and orientation of the tracked patient inside the coordinate system of the camera. In most cases it is desired to have the position of the tracked probe, converted to a position and orientation relative to the patient, i.e. in the coordinate system of the patient. Here $M_W TL$ is the matrix multiplication $M_W T^{-1} \dot{M}_T L$. A third patient transformation often required is that from the patient, to the computer generated image (i.e. CT or MRI data) $M_P W$. It is then possible to visualise the tracked tool relative to the image data, through the matrix multiplication $M_W TL^- 1 \dot{M}_P W$.

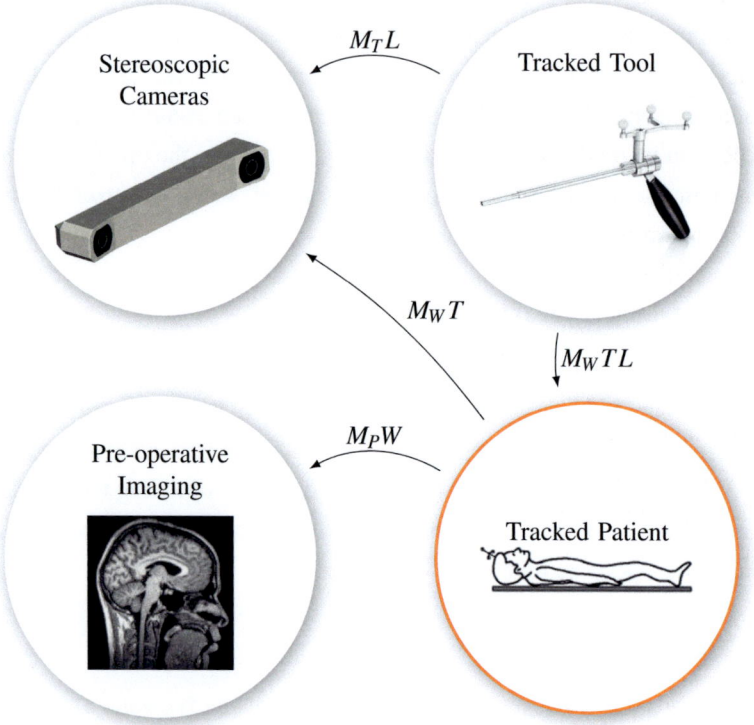

Figure 2.9.: Coordinate System Transformation Matrixes

2.2.6. Patient Registration

Registration is a key problem in medical imaging because the surgeon must often compare or fuse different images or, in the case of surgical navigation, they need to have the exact alignment between the preoperative and the current patient's position. The perfect overlapping of a virtual dataset and reality is a rigid registration problem. There are many different methods in literature but only two are predominantly applied in practice, these are the surface based registration technique and the point based registration technique. The latter is also called landmark based registration. From section 2.2.5 this is the determination of the $M_P W$ term.

Point based registration correlates natural or artificial points from the pre-operative imaging to the patient. The chosen points are readily identifiable in both the pre-operative imaging, as well as on the patient in the OR. Natural points chosen can include landmark features such as the tip of the nose, or artificial landmarks such as inserted titanium screws. The use of titanium screws for a point-to-point registration is termed as the 'Gold Standard' for accuracy[29]. For this registration, the pointer requires its own matrix that defines the offset of the point tip from the position and orientation returned by the optical tracking camera. This is normally achieved through a process called pivotisation. Pivoting involves fixing the tip of the pointer at a single place, and then rotating the pointer around this one point. The collection of points and orientations obtained by the optical tracking camera form a section of a surface of a sphere. The center of this sphere will be found at the place of orientation. This process is shown in Figure 2.10. Because this process inherently includes errors, it is often also used during the registration procedure. Instead of measuring the single point returned by the optical tracking cameras, it is preferable to 'pivot' about the point to be measured, getting a multitude of measurements from a variety of orientations, and averaging these measurements out.

The second type of registration is surface scanning. This method acquires surface data from the patient in the operating theatre to calculate an alignment to the segmented pre-operative imagery. Data can be acquired with a tracked laser scanner or with a complete laser surface scanner that is also tracked[48]. This method collects hundreds to thousands of points; however, because the scan is from the soft tissue of the patient, that can

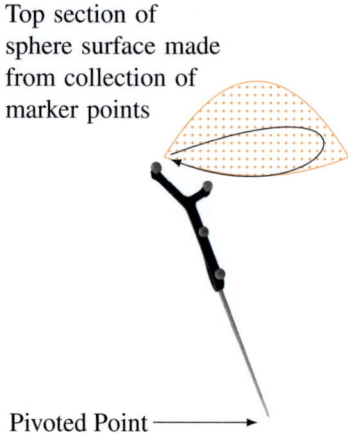

Top section of
sphere surface made
from collection of
marker points

Pivoted Point ⟶

Figure 2.10.: Pivotisation with Optically Tracked Tool

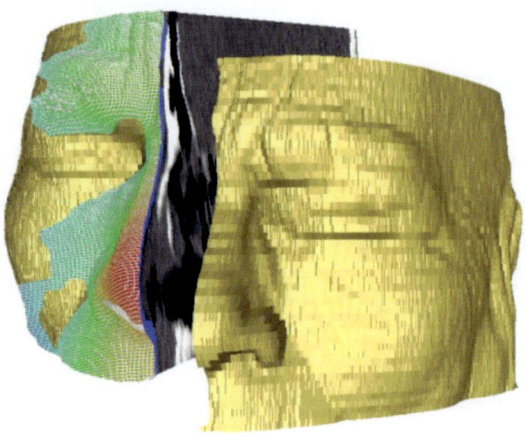

Figure 2.11.: Example of laser scan data registered and overlayed on matching CT
data.

move slightly between pre-operative and the operating room, there is often a slightly higher error[77]. An example of this registration method is shown in Figure 2.11.

2.3. Mobile Robotics Grounding

Mobile Robots are employed extensively commercially in industry, as well as targets of research. The term of Mobile Robotics covers any robot that is able to move its own position, this can be with wheels, legs or any other movement concept. The robot can be fully autonomous, but this is not necessary. A mobile robot may also be semi-autonomous receiving commands through radio or wire, and at the other extreme can be completely human controlled as a teleoperations platform.

Mobile Robots have already been employed in the medical area as transport devices for medicine or specimens within a hospital, as a mobility assistant machines for rehabilitation, and even as a mobile toilet system for elderly people[124]. Presently the use of mobile robotics in precision critical applications in surgery is non-existent. This area of robotics has been the domain of large modified industrial robots where their high degree of precision is of the greatest benefit. Many other smaller and novel systems have arisen through the years, and have been given the title of Steady Hand Surgical Assistants. Examples as early as 1999 by Taylor et al. [123] presented the concept for reducing hand tremors and for overcoming human sensorimotor limitations. However, the side-effect for using the smaller systems, was a smaller work space available on the patient.

2.3.1. Kinematics of Wheeled Mobile Robots

Specific to this thesis are the sub-group of mobile robots, the wheeled mobile robots (WMRs). The kinematics of WMRs are highly dependent on the wheel layout and of which wheels in the layout are actively driven. Figure 2.12 provides a generalised description of these constraints. While a comprehensive overview of the development and classification of different kinds of WMR can be found elsewhere [[17][27][81][83]], three examples are given here:

1. A Bicycle. Includes one active driven wheel directly behind a second non-driven, but steerable wheel.

2. A Car. Includes two driven wheels on one axle directly behind two non-driven, but steerable wheels.

3. A Tank. Includes two co-axial driven treads, no passive wheels and no steered wheels. The driven treads could be approximated to two very large wheels with a significantly long surface contact area.

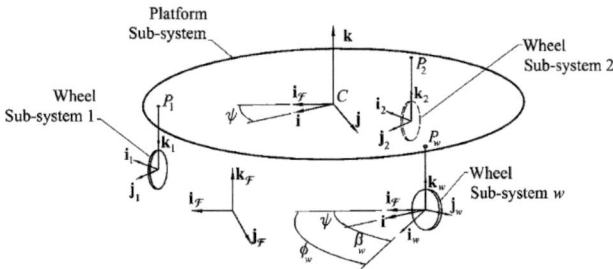

Figure 2.12.: Generalised Description of WMR Kinematic Parameters, from [73]

This last type of WMR is also termed more specifically a WMR with unicycle kinematics. They can have additional passive wheels for stability, but importantly, they have only two driven wheels coaxially located and not steered. There are several design methodologies for defining the exact kinematics of the robots, using the differential model, or through the Jacobian to relate the motion of the wheels to the robot. The choice of the kinematic definition influences strongly the type of control available, or the complexity of control required to be implemented to avoid singularities.

In the common approach to the kinematic model of a Unicycle WMR will only have two control inputs, being the rotational velocities of the left

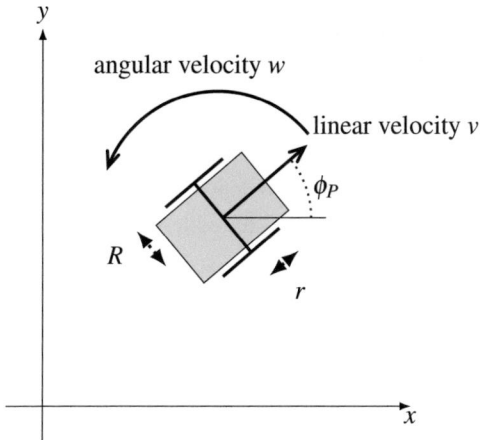

Figure 2.13.: Unicycle Kinematic Parameter Definitions

and right wheels, w_1 and w_2. These can be directly related the forward velocity v and rotational velocities w of the robot by equation 2.2, where r is the radius of the wheels and R is the half the distance between the two wheels. Unfortunately, the kinematics as popularly viewed here is limited to 2D. Additional 3D analysis of WMR in literature is limited to specific constraints such as the effect of tilted wheels on slippage.

$$
w_1 = \frac{v - Rw}{r}
$$
$$
w_2 = \frac{v + Rw}{r} \tag{2.2}
$$

2.3.2. Control of Wheeled Mobile Robots

Much of the first research for control of Unicycle robots and more widely WMRs was based on geometric methods. Examples from Ollero [91] used circular arcs and Shin [108] used fifth order polynomials. However, these methods are principally based on point to point trajectory tracking and it is often difficult to guarantee stability for such a system. Errors in early trajectories can propagate through to later trajectories. It is more apt here to thus investigate the actual line following robots. Very simple robots can here be implemented without any significant control algorithm at all, only a sensor array detecting the 'line' and boolean logic for the motor control. Such systems have even been demonstrated applicable for school groups attempting to enter robotics. However, with any such approach, there is no possibility of achieving a stable or smooth movement, two key elements required later for precision.

3. State of the Art

As covered in the previous chapter, the required application here sees the meeting of two distinct areas. Firstly, the continually emerging and developing area of medical robotics, and secondly the well grounded area of Mobile Robotics including all of its required study of kinematics, control mechanisms and studies of its operating characteristics in areas such as overcoming friction, or overcoming system noise inputs. To date there is no application that has attempted to bridge the gap between these two areas, and as such the state of the art in this chapter provides a series of short overviews of research projects from the first area, previous research attempts for performing Robotic and Computer Assisted Surgery for Craniotomies or other closely related medical applications. The emphasis here is on the ability to transfer the precision of the preplanning into the operating room. Included is this summary is a third area that is similar to this bridge, that being hand-held surgical robots or steady hand assistants. While not all of these robots do not attempt to perform Craniotomies with a planning transfer solution, they are worthy of study for their similarity with lessons to be learned in areas such as engineered sterilised solutions etc.

Additionally relevant to the state of the art for surgical robotics includes the basis concepts from Image Guided Surgery. These concepts and technologies, such as Tracking Systems and Registration Techniques etc, are relevant to the State of the Art, but here are considered assumed knowledge. While it is accepted that these concepts and technologies will be built on and used in this project, it is not expected that they will be specifically targeted for improvement and as such are not discussed here any further than what was already offered in the Scientific Grounding of the last chapter.

3.1. State of the Art in Robotic Solutions for Craniotomy Surgeries

Presented here is the current state of the art in each of these sub-sections of Image Guided Surgery, as well as two current robotic solutions for Craniotomy Surgeries using varied approaches from the IGS philosophies.

3.1.1. Robocka

Robocka[32] is a work completed by Engel et al. at the Karlsruhe University Institute of Process Control and Robotics in collaboration with the Oral- and Cranio-Maxillofacial Surgery department of the Ruprecht-Karls-University Hospital Heidelberg. This system was based on the previous Casper robot system with additional safety components integrated. The system was developed for the purpose of Craniotomies at the bony skull and was the first system that actually performed milling trajectories on patients with permanently changing positions and orientations of the tool piece.

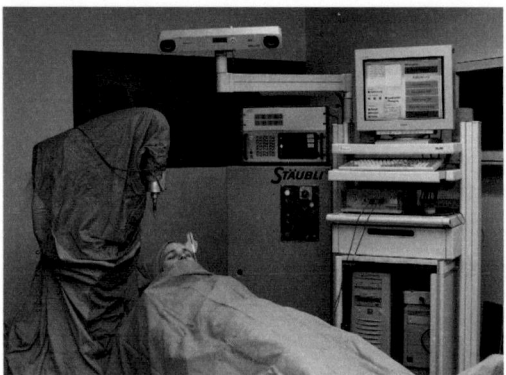

Figure 3.1.: Robocka

3.1.2. Crigos

In the work completed by Bast et al.[7], the Crigos system was built employing a parallel kinematic hexapod system beneath the patients head with a large structure used to hold the tool over the patients head. The system was designed for Craniotomies, and specifically the resection of cranial tumours. One shortfall of this system is the lack of ability to change the tool orientation, which must be set before the commencement of surgery, and cannot be changed without re-registration of the tool tip. This significantly reduced the workspace of the Crigos. As such, it was not able to complete single step Craniotomys for procedures such as Frontal Orbital advancement; however, it was quite capable of cutting accurate implant beds for positioning of dental or surgical implants.

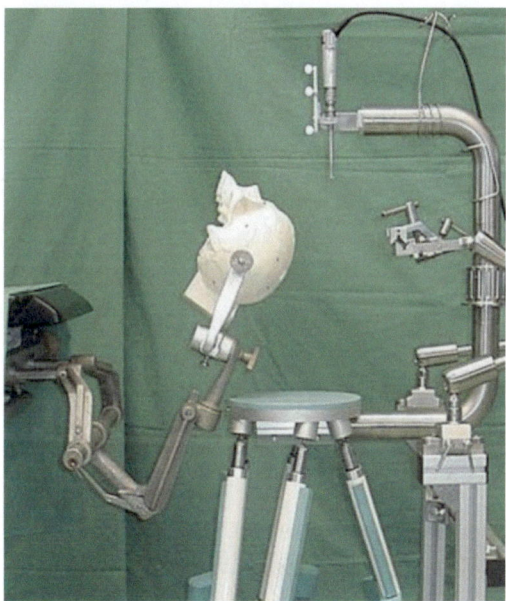

Figure 3.2.: Crigos

3.1.3. AccuRobAs

A system currently being developed by the IPR, Karlsruhe, named AccuRobAs is a new concept for achieving a robot assisted craniotomy with the use of a CO_2 laser. Outlined in the initial works by Burgner et al. [15], the work demonstrates a potential for achieving very high accuracy, thin craniotomy cuts over complex trajectories. A cut is suggested to be only 400μm wide. The use of a laser also provides a significant medical advantage that the system does not require physical contact with the patient, therefore ensuring the sterilised nature of the operations site. However, this work in progress has three significant disadvantages. Firstly, there is not presently any method for detecting when the laser cutting achieves breakthrough of the bone. This means the system in it's current state has too great a risk for causing permanent brain injury by cutting too deep. Secondly, the system is very slow. CO_2 laser ablation of bone is a pulsed process, with up to 200Hz, each pulse removing a volume from a half ellipsoid with 200μm diameter, but with only 50μm depth. A complete ablation can take an hour or more. Work by Mehrwald et al. [82] attempts to reduce this processing time of bone ablation by pre-ablation soaking or coating of the bone with mixtures of glycerin or a glycerin water mix. The higher melting point of the glycerin results in a larger ablation volume per pulse. Unfortunately, it is not yet known if an improvement in the overall processing time can be achieved or if the required soaking time (up to 10mins) is counter beneficial.

3.1.4. Additional works

Other works worthy of mention, are the extension of these osteotomy machines to include Torque Sensor based control for the Surgeon. Acrobot[79] for example uses a 5 DOF constraint, with the Surgeon moving the robot anywhere within the safe area. The robot providing a virtual fixtures concept. This concept is similar in application to the PADyC robot by

Troccaz et al. [104] except that the PADyC used a 6 DOF constraint that was based on passive clutches that would admit motions if they would not break the positioning constraints.

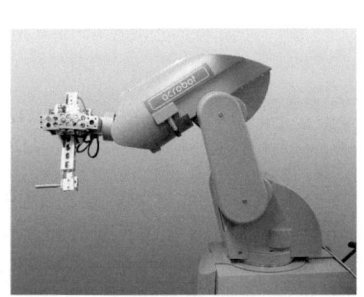

Figure 3.3.: Acrobot

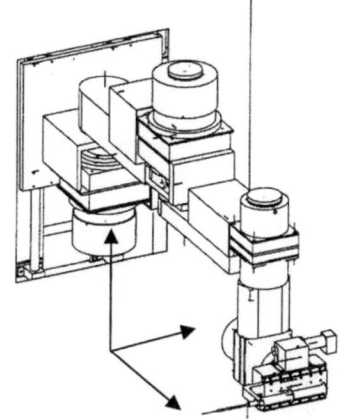

Figure 3.4.: PADyC

3.2. State of the Art in Handheld Surgical Robots / Tools

Here we look at three examples of handheld surgical tools. The first is the Intelligent Tool Drive (ITD), the second is the Precision Freehand Sculptor (PFS), and the third which is possibly the closest similar project to this planned here, is the Sicherheits-Trepanationssystems (STS).

3.2.1. Intelligent Tool Drive (ITD)

The Intelligent Tool Drive (ITD) [96] is a handheld tool designed to improve the accuracy of Surgeons in performing the drilling stage of a spinal pedical placement. The concept involves the use of a handheld hexapod in replacement to a 6-DOF industrial robot, with all the concepts discussed in the above section on Surgical Robotics. Through constant tracking using an optical twin camera system, the ITD intends to keep a surgical tool at the correct position, angle and pressure, through the movement of the parallel kinematic system.

The system minimises the impact of the robot to the OR, and offers a flexible mounting plate that can attach to a number of different tools; however, a significant constraint of the system appears to be the weight of the actuated system. The system has not yet been demonstrated in a hand-held roll. Figure 4 is a cropped photo of the robot held in a metal frame, shown briefly at the bottom of the picture.

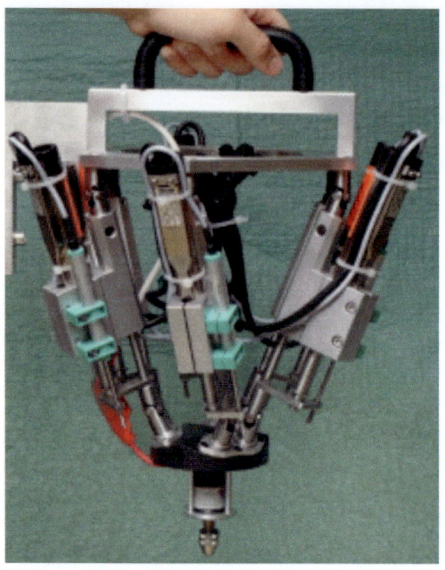

Figure 3.5.: The Intelligent Tool Drive, Developed by Mannheim Hospital

3.2.2. Precision Freehand Sculptor (PFS)

The Precision Freehand Sculptor (PFS)[12] supports the surgeon in performing accurate osteotomies for placement of knee implants. The tool is tracked as the surgeon moves the tool over the desired osteotomy area. The cutting tool is continually spinning but is withdrawn into the tool should the tool move over an area that should not be cut. The use of this for implant preparation is good as it allows minimum impact on the surgeons workflow, he/she is entirely in control of the device, but safety guards are provided through the tool. Unfortunately its adaption to trajectory cutting is slightly limited because the surgeon would have to move the tool back and forth continually over the trajectory line as the tool cuts only a little each pass. This would lead to a significant slowing of the procedure being conducted.

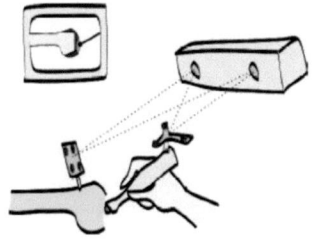

Figure 3.6.: The Precision Freehand Sculptor (PFS) Concept

Figure 3.7.: PFS Clutch Tool (left) and shaver tool (right)

3.2.3. Sicherheits-Trepenationssystems (STS)

The Sicherheits-Trepenationssystems (STS)[40] (RWTH, Aachen University, Aachen, Germany) is a handheld tool to improve the safety of craniotomy procedures. While the system does not offer any guidance to the cutting trajectory, it does offer some intriguing embedded sensor technology in a handheld device that is worthy of note here.

The STS is designed as a safe-guard to prevent excessive cutting depth in the process of a craniotomy. The handheld device uses three actuated legs to control the cutting depth and lean / tilt of the tool. The system's strength lies in the use of integrated ultra-sonic sensors embedded in these legs. The ultra-sonic sensors are used to provide updated and exacting information of the skull depth directly beneath the legs.

While this concept is outlined in the projects website, the project has not yet demonstrated the capability of the integrated sensors. The project also plans a change from a standard boring Craniotomy drill piece to use a new special tissue sparing tool. However, in the papers presented to date, a Craniotomy drill piece is used in the tests of tool angle control. Apart from these two points, which still are not yet proven; the system offers no additional capability above Optical Image Tracking, and Image Guided Surgery. One major shortfall of the system appears to be that the surrounding of the tool with the actuated legs, prevents the surgeon seeing the actual surgical location.

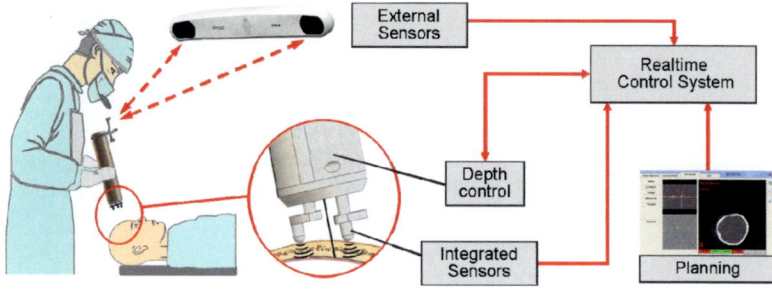

Figure 3.8.: The Sicherheits-Trepenationssystems (STS) Concept

3.3. Discussion from Medical Robotics State of the Art

There is clearly a gap in the middle of these areas, with development to bridge the gap requiring advances to be made in many areas. When looking at the previous research efforts we can see the improvements that need to be made. The previous robot systems are very large and cumbersome, bringing significant impact on the Operating Room.

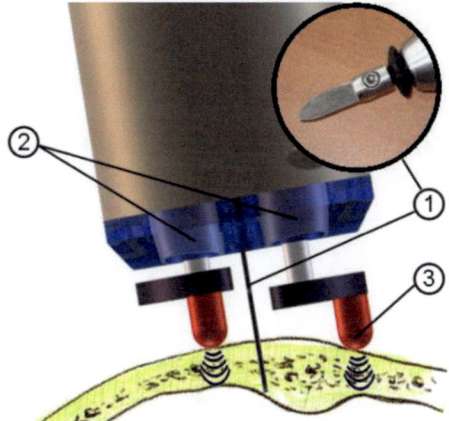

Figure 3.9.: STS Tool end, showing (1) the cutting tool, (2) the actuated legs to control depth and angle, (3) the tip of the leg with included sensors.

The Steady Hand Surgical Assistants on the other hand, are significantly limited in their capability, but have one strong advantage of ensuring the surgeon stays in control of the operation.

The one system that has made an attempt to cross between these two areas would be the ITD. But the work has still resulted in a system that is considerably large and ungainly, too heavy and unpractical to be employed by a surgeon. One other point to watch is that the STS, as an attempt to make a hand-held craniotomy tool, has resulted in a tool with limited visibility to the surgical site.

To summarise this chapter, the Tables 3.1 and 3.2 includes the main strengths and weaknesses of each system.

Table 3.1.: Comparison between different Surgical Robot research projects

	Strengths	Weaknesses
Robocka	Accurate System that was used in a clinical trial.	Very large system using Rx-90 Robot. System was not trusted in clinical trial to completely penetrate skull. Still required surgeon to complete the craniotomy by hand.
Crigos	Hexapod kinematic is highly accurate and stable, system did not impact greatly on operating room as majority of robot fitted underneath operating table.	Limited Rotation capability in kinematics, requires multiple steps to complete trajectory.
AccuRobAs	Flexible System Strucutre and Concept with non-contact CO_2 laser cutting, capable of complex trajectories	Very slow processing of bone, Very large impact on Operating Room
Acrobot	Force Controlled System, Surgeon completely in control for freehand bone removal.	Very large system.
PADyC	Force Controlled System, can hold variety of tools, can be wall mounted or roof mounted to minimise impact on OP.	Very large system depite no active links.

Table 3.2.: Comparison between different Surgical Tool Assistant projects

	Strengths	Weaknesses
ITD	Fast parallel kinematic structure and drive	Very large system that is heavy to carry and impractical for the surgeon to support for long period of time.
PFS	Small Compact Device.	Slow disengaging of clutch could allow bone processing outside safety zone
STS	Small Compact Device, 3 included degrees of freedom, intrinsic and extrinsic sensing	No ability to track a trajectory. Limited visibility to the surgical site.

4. Design Concept

The following chapter provides the background to the chosen design. The search for a new robot concept was initially quite broad and not restricted to a wheeled mobile robot. This idea search was completed after the completion of stage 1 of the Engineering Requirements analysis was completed. From these requirements, such details of required work area, speeds, forces were known, and a series of ideas were scoped for the required design.

4.1. Idea Searching

One concept followed heavily in the idea searching was the use of the skull itself for relative positioning. Instead of a large industrial robot with stability gained through rigidity. It was thought that the positioning of a smaller hand-held or position-supporting robot could achieve the same or better result. To this extent, all possible robot mechanisms were analysed to see how they could be applied in this manner to achieve the intended drilling. This chapter therefore looks at all possibilities for achieving such a robot, then limits the scope but extends to evaluate three possible ideas.

4.1.1. Mobile Robot Possibilities

All possible movement mechanisms were analysed using a comparison to nature, using animals and other moving items. In this approach three distinct robot concepts were examined further.

The options for the hyper-redundant snake like robot was immediately discounted due to the problem having no requirement to navigate confined

Table 4.1.: Possible movement mechanisms for a mobile robot

Inspirational Object	Mechanism	Similar Mechanism	Technical Implemenation
Cat	Walking	Crawling	Walking Robot
Bird	Flying	Hovering	
Car	Rolling	Rotating	Wheeled or tracked Robot
Lizard	Creeping	Wriggling	Crawling Robot
Snake	Slithering, Rocking, Wiggling	Winding	Hyper-redundant Serial Link Robot
Kangaroo	Hopping, Jumping	Pushing off	
Fish	Swimming	Diving	

chambers or tunnels and the use of such a robot would have created un-neccessary complexities. The walking robot was seen as a special case of the Swinging robot concept, without the parallel kinematic structures being fixed, and thus losing the main advantages of this concept. This left three concepts that were examined further.

1. A creeping robot - that clamps on two or more positions of the skull, and alternately moves each clamped position.

2. A swinging robot - that uses a series of anchor points on the skull, and moves an end effector through parallel actuators.

3. A mobile, wheeled robot - that grips and moves across the skull relative to the required trajectory.

4.2. Creeping Robot

This concept was developed to show the nature of using the grip on the skull with a developed motion based on that of a creeping caterpillar. The concept is shown in Figure 4.1, with the developed moving concept shown in Figure 4.2. The abstraction show is only used to explain one possible evolution of the design, and many other possible interpretations of this concept are possible. This section will shortly explain this model, how the movement is achieved, and how the cutting is controlled. The robot shown in Figure 4.1 requires a minimum of 5 actuated controls for the motion. Two translational actuators (Active Links 1 and 3) operate the clamps, that can stop any slippage of the robot. Two passive rotational links (Passive links 1 and 2) allow the system to bend over curved surfaces, and comply with the movement of Active Link 2, which is used to drive the robot forwards. As one possible alternate solution Active Link 2 can be replaced with a translational link directly between Passive Links 1 and 2. A final rotational joint allows the movement of the drilling arm in the xy plane. Additional controls could include adding tilt, lean and a z axis control to the drilling arm, or replacing the translational clamp links with passive loaded plates that are designed to slide in only one direction.

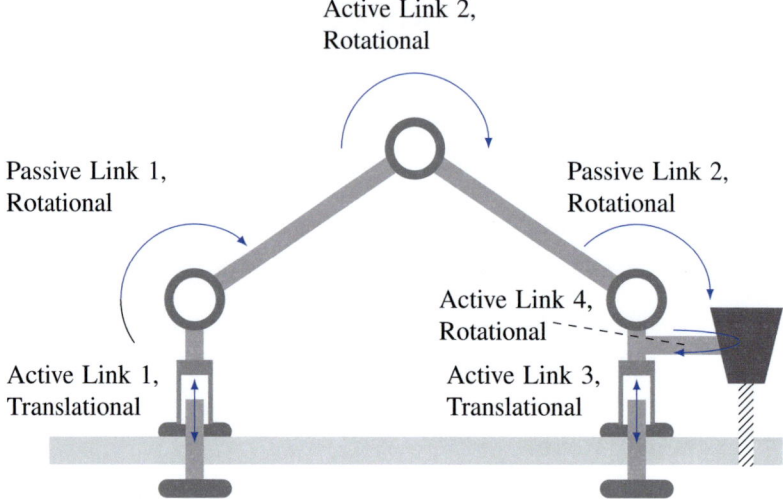

Figure 4.1.: Concept for Caterpillar design

4.2.1. Creeping Motion

The movement in Figure 4.2 and explained here shows robot moving to the right. This movement commences with the use of the translational actuated clamps. After fixing the front clamp and releasing the rear clamp in Figure 4.2a, step 2 then involves the shortening of the distance between the front and back legs. Because only the front leg is clamped, this means the rear leg is pulled forwards. In Step 3, the clamp positions are reversed, and the middle actuator reverses, thus expanding the distance between the front and back legs. With the reversed clamp positions, the front leg is pushed forwards. At this stage, the steering must occur. The pushing forwards of the front leg, also pushes forwards the drill. By moving the drill rotationally around the front leg, the channel that is cut, and hence the path that the front leg follows, can be modified. With a section of the trajectory cut, the clamps are reversed again, and the motion continues.

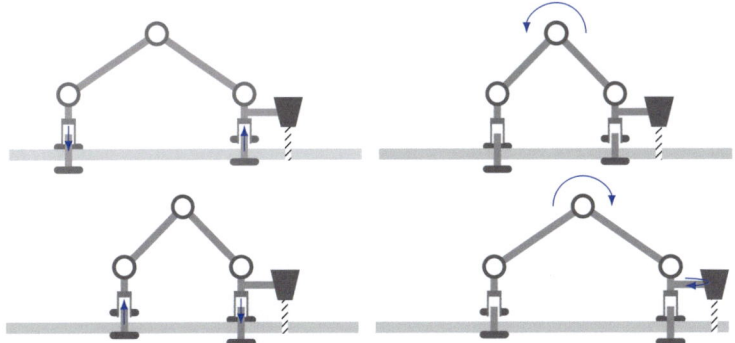

Figure 4.2.: Concept for Caterpillar Movement with Drilling

4.2.2. Creeping Robot Summary

In brainstorming, the robot yielded several distinct advantages. Firstly, the system offers a very good refined control on the robots movement. The two clamping arms are separated an adequate distance to allow a good level of torque to be used for moving the cutting arm positioned forward. The clamps can use any amount of force desired to ensure grip, with no threat of damaging soft tissue. The clamps also have the additional advantage of being able to separate the Dura Matter themselves, and also their use prevents any bone flap from being pushed into the skull, thus improving the safety of the entire operation. The system was however discounted for a few reasons. Complexities were seen with the initial insertion of the clamps, that would either require a large entry whole, or a complex folding mechanism that is risky for insertion into a patients skull. Additionally it was noted that the system had an inevitable autonomous nature for control, with no hands-on control concept being identified. Finally, because the overall movement involved a single push from a rear position, there lies no ability to cut trajectories with sharp corners. In an example case of attempting a near 90 degrees turn, when the front robot leg has advanced against the corner, it would no longer be able to 'push' the front leg forward, but instead would be required to apply a torque to twist this front leg 'sideways'. This is not impossible, but would require again a further degree of control.

While for these reasons, this concept was discounted from further analysis in this project, it remains a possible project for future study. This future study can pursue applications not only on hard surfaces but additionally for soft tissues, such as the stomach lining, where the clamping nature of the device can independently hold the separated flaps together, and hold the robot on vertical surfaces. Finally identified here were industrial applications that allow the cutting of items such as sheet metal in difficult to reach locations.

4.3. Swinging Robot

The swinging robot was viewed in a concept of a parallel kinematics robot. The robot utilises two or more anchor points on the skull. The anchor points would be titanium screws similar to those used for standard IGS registration. Connecting to these anchor points, a series of linear or rotational actuators or passive clutches can be used to position the Craniotomy tool piece. The anchor points would be placed in a similar manner to that of registration screws, prior to surgery, and prior to imaging. By mounting the robot directly to the anchor points, whose locations are known from prior imagery, there is no requirement for intra-operative registration.

4.3.1. Parallel Kinematics Machines (PKMs)

In contrast to serial kinematics, parallel kinematics are generally thought of to develop systems that are more accurate and with greater stiffness for a machining tool. This statement however requires clarification. Analysis has now indicated that stiffness of a hexapod (one of the most common

PKMs and generally reflective of the field) is very sensitive to its location in the workspace, and indeed the stiffness and accuracy rapidly drops as the spindle moves away from the "sweet spot" of the machine. This increase of stiffness and accuracy is also not without compromise. The increasing of complexities within the kinematics and control of parallel kinematic machines induces a loss of manipulability through a greater number of singularities and reversals that complicate trajectory movement and their inherent control within the workspace.

A further complication of parallel kinematic machines is the increased number of joints. A 6 DOF serial machine requires 6 actuated joints; whereas a 5 DOF hexapod requires 6 actuated telescopic struts, 6 spherical joints and 6 universal joints. Every joint brings additional compliance that adds up to decrease the overall system stability. Because of the duality of the serial / parallel debate, many researchers have pushed in favour of a hybrid design, avoiding the pitfalls of both. For this reason, both a parallel system and a hybrid system are proposed here.

4.3.2. System Requirements

In order to achieve the positioning of the drill on the skull, the degrees of freedom are analysed to determine the required robot. The trajectory is defined as a series of points in 3D, however, if the system is able to use the fact they are sitting on the skull surface, this can be reduced to a non-linear 2D. The twist of the drill is not relevant, leaving only two degrees of lean and tilt, relevant. In comparing the possible modes here, most designs with linear actuators were discounted because of the accepted spherical nature of the skull. It is nearly impossible to use a linear actuator, anchored at one point on the skull, reaching over the skull and to any other desired point on the skull. Thus the effort here is concentrated on the use of the RR(R) kinematic schemas. There are here two main possibilities, either the rotational joints are positioned vertically (arching over the skull), or horizontally (around the skull). Both concepts have distinct disadvantages, when determining the build space for links that arching over the skull, it was found a large amount of space was taken away from the surgeon, restricting his / her grip of the end-effector, and also restricting visibility of the surgical site. Placing the links around the skull frees up the surgical site, but requires the head to be positioned (and held) with very little support throughout the surgery. This was firstly seen as unpractical for the surgeons who move the head often during the surgery as the craniotomy proceeds, but it was also noted that the links are thus placed in a plane perpendicular to the drilling axis. This has another disadvantage that all the drilling torques directly affect the accuracy of the joint control (this was also found previously in industrial applications). For this reason, machining applications are preferably parallel kinematics with linear actuators, but already mentioned here is that these linear actuators are not acceptable. An alternate possibility for the rotational link positioning, is to enable a passive third degree of freedom, allowing the plane of rotation of the joints to be moved, similar to a redundant 7th degree of freedom in a serial kinematic design. This option increases the complexity of the kinematics and mechanical design requirements, and is viewed as a future development, though not pursued in greater detail here.

4.3.3. Remote Centre of Motion (RCM)

All general mechanisms for both serial or parallel kinematic machines are made up of parts and joints. If a part of the mechanism can rotate around a fixed point distal within the coordinate system of the mechanism, but without any physical revolute joint at the desired fixed point, then this mechanism may be called a remote center of motion (RCM) mechanisms[31].

The RCM mechanisms were initially developed to position and manipulate tools or endoscopes in some minimally invasive surgery (MIS) or surgery robotic applications. During MIS, surgical tools or trocars (cm size) pass through small incisions to reach the surgical site. The entry point as a kinematical constraint acts as a pivot that the tools have to be moved in a spherical configuration. The introduction of RCM mechanisms in MIS provides a fixed entry point (coincided with RCM point) of the endoscope into the patients body during the whole operation process, enhances safety and quality of the surgery, and gives facilities for surgeons. Such mechanisms have been used widely in robot assisted surgery applications, such as the wrist module of Da Vinci surgical system [2]. In fact, almost all commercially endoscope surgical robots are RCM-based robots.

Here it is intended to use this principle for a different purpose. The desired trajectory lies on the surface of the skull. While this surface is not spherical, it is the closest approximation of the surface to a standard coordinate system. The intent here is thus to use a 1-DOF rotational RCM for each parallel link to place the centre of the RCM near to the centre of the patients head. Any movement of the rotational links, makes the end effector movement approximately spherical in nature, thus the final required adjustment according to the skull surface is minimized. This final movement in a z axis perpendicular to the skull surface is achieved with a single passive ball joint at the anchor points.

4.3.4. Kinematic Schemas and possible solutions

Two possible concepts for achieving this design, one is a hybrid parallel serial kinematic. The system uses two RR arms in parallel for positioning, and two direct drive links for setting the tilt and lean of the drill.

The second possible design uses two parallel kinematic solutions. The first system uses four RR arms in parallel, for positioning and orientating the drill. The second is in the RTRT configuration.

For both designs we can let X be the same end effector configuration, with Θ the active joint angles of the machine, which are specified by 4-

tuples.

$$X = [A\ B\ \phi\ \lambda]^T \tag{4.1}$$

$$\Theta = [\theta_1\ \theta_2\ \theta_3\ \theta_4]^T \tag{4.2}$$

where A and B are used for the two coordinate notations inside the workspace on the surface (not cartesian x and y), ϕ and λ represent the tilt and lean of the robot with respect to the perpendicular of the skull. The relationship between X and Θ can be written as

$$F(X,\Theta) = 0 \tag{4.3}$$

where $F : R^4 \times R^4 \to R^4$. By differentiating 4.3 with respect to time we have

$$F_X \dot{X} + F_\Theta \dot{\Theta} = 0 \tag{4.4}$$

where $F_X = \delta F/\delta X$ and $F_\Theta = \delta F/\delta \Theta$.

If F_X is not singular, the Jacobian matrix, J, of the mechanism which is useful for investigating kinematic properties, such as manipulability, kinematic and actuator singularities of the mechanism, can be obtained by using F_X and F_Θ in Eq.

$$J(X,\Theta) = -F_X^{-1} F_\Theta \tag{4.5}$$

so that $\dot{X} = J\dot{\Theta}$. Likewise, we define, $J^{-1} = -F_\Theta^{-1} F_X$, when F_Θ is not singular. When $|F_X|$ or $|F_\Theta|$ becomes zero, the structure experiences either kinematic or actuator singularities.

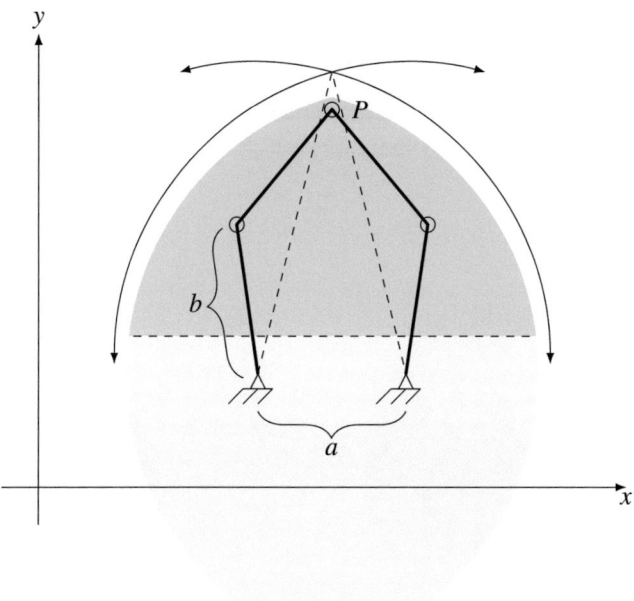

Figure 4.3.: Approximate Workspace of PKM in 2D plane, P is end effector position

4.3.5. Reachability

To determine if singularities could be a problem with such a design, the reachability of such a design over the workspace was analysed. This involved initially only for the 2D case, later extended to the 3D case with the RCM. Design constraints included symmetrical arms, with length b and offset across a base distance of a. Such a design is shown in Figure 4.3. Logic here assumes that control must dictate both arms bend outwards, away from the skull. From this figure we can see that the workable space (with a safety factor included after taking into consideration planar collisions and joint limitations) can be approximated to an ellipse (complete grey area) with sides $2b - \delta$ and the base $4b - a - \delta$.

This base spread is also relevant for the stability of the joint control. The

47

kinematics actually allow this workspace to occur forwards and backwards of the base positions. However, in order to avoid complications discussed in the previous section in control through singularities and collisions, only a single half is considered (dark grey area).

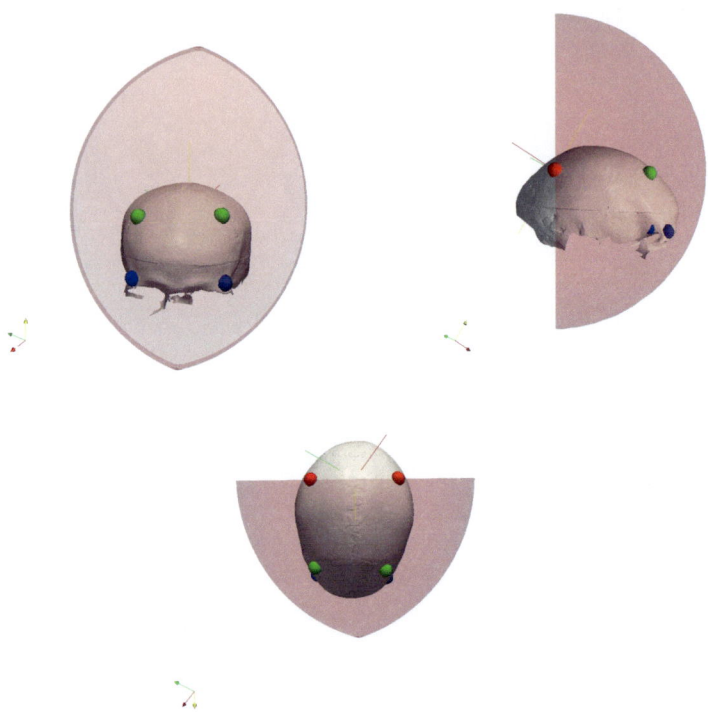

Figure 4.4.: Approximate working volume of PKM overlayed on sample skull

To make a rough approximation of whether such a concept would provide acceptable coverage to a skull, the workspace projection was extended to 3D with a series of sample marker / anchor positions used (two red markers in Figure 4.4 were used here on the parietal bone). The possible working volume in this example using a sample adult skull is shown as the transparent red area. For this example the baseline was 100mm. Complete coverage (100% volume of skull encased in working volume of PKM) was found with symmetric arm lengths of 90mm. However, this concept does not take into account any collisions with the skull. Clearly the maximum reach cannot be achieved to the front of the skull with straight arm segments. To view any modification that may be made, a series of cross sections were made through the above views, centered on the axis of the anchors, indicating the planes that the system could swing between. These are shown in Figure 4.5.

There are a number of different ways to avoid or manage this collision issue. Figure 4.6a shows one idea as the extension of the developed tool holder. By extending the tool holder laterally, the normal PKM straight links would abstractly go around the skull. However, by separating the end points of the two parallel arms, this concept extends the degrees of freedom for the design with the orientation of the tool holder unrestricted. This then requires a further active joint in order to achieve a stable controllable solution. Another possible solution is shown in Figure 4.6 and replaces the straight PKM links with curved arm segments. This approach was then pursued through collision checking to see if a 100% coverage is still possible. This time not with the volume of the skull, but instead with the surface of the skull.

Figure 4.7 shows the outcome of this analysis using the same parameters as before, (100mm baseline, and 90mm long segments of curved arms). The 90mm length was the end point to end point straight line length, and not the curved segment length. Seen in Figure 4.7 the achievable workspace is shown as the combination of the yellow and dark blue regions. The light blue region shows an area not achievable with the right parietal bone based link, and the green area shows that not achievable with the left parietal bone based link (The anchor points, identical to the previous example are shown here as black markers). With this collision analysis we see that a

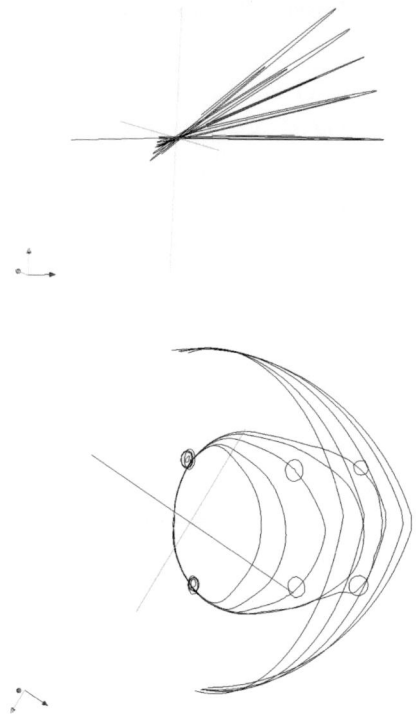

Figure 4.5.: Cross Sections through working volume of PKM with sample skull

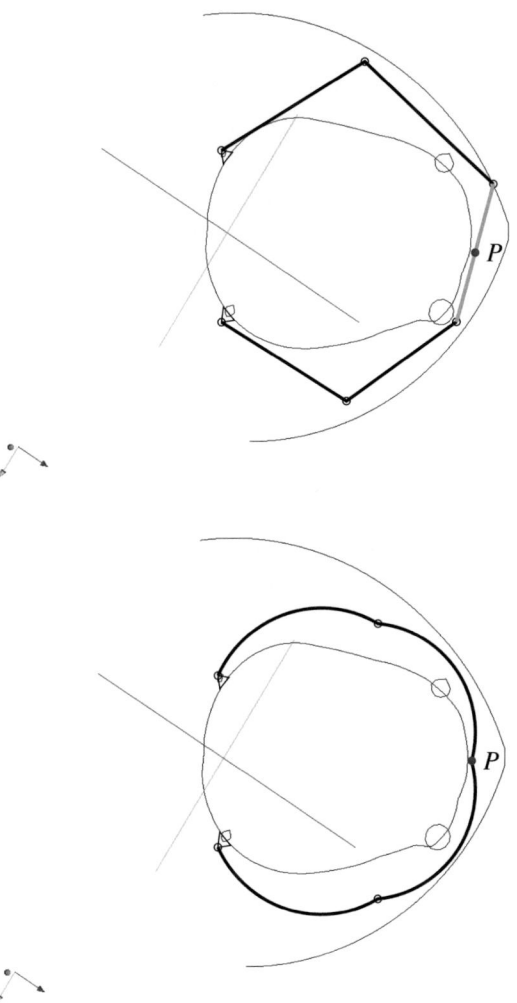

Figure 4.6.: Collision Avoidance Solutions

100% coverage is no longer possible with the 90mm lengths of the previous example. However, when this same calculations are repeated with 100mm lengths, a near 100% coverage is possible. This coverage is shown in Figure 4.8. With these arms it is possible to achieve coverage to all the parietal bone, frontal bone, supraorbital foramen and process. However, coverage cuts short in the lateral orbital regions. Arm lengths of 105mm were then found to be acceptable in achieving a 100% coverage after collision.

4.3.6. Control of the PKM

The solution described above uses two active joints to control the position-ing of the robot on the skull, and two active joints to control the angle and lean of the drill. This is an underconstrained problem where the surface of the skull can be considered as the third constraint. It is possible to view the surface of the skull in terms of a 2 component coordinate system (as was the original equation 4.1) $[AB]^T$. However, the second two components of $[\phi \; \lambda]^T$ have non-linear dependencies on the full 3 degrees of the surface.

While only two active joints are required to drive this system in all three dimensions, it is here that the collision with the skull of the tool tip (or an appropriate designed stopper) sets up our the 3rd degree. However, this implies that equation 4.5 was not adequate in solving the system. In this case, the problem was that equation 4.1 describes only the surface in a co-ordinate system $[AB]^T$ and not in terms of $[xyz]^T$. To this extent, it would be required to map between the two coordinate systems. This could be achieved using the pre-operative data, inclusive of marker positions, to cal-culate the mapping. This would then be used as a feed-forward term in the jacobian. Starting with the expansion of 4.5 we have

$$[\dot{\Theta}_1 \; \dot{\Theta}_2 \; \dot{\Theta}_3 \; \dot{\Theta}_4]^T = J^{-1}[\dot{A} \; \dot{B} \; \dot{\phi} \; \dot{\lambda}]^T \qquad (4.6)$$

but including the proposed feedforward term we would need

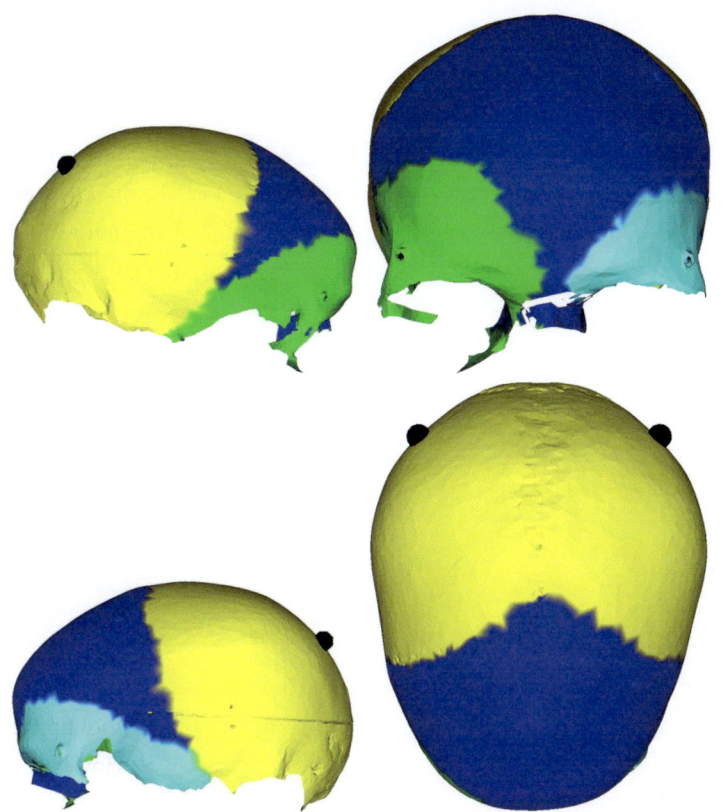

Figure 4.7.: Achievable workspace on skull, with collision analysis for two 90mm curved arms, hinged by spherical joints at anchor points (black). Yellow is reachable, but with high likelihood of singularity problems in control. Dark Blue is reachable and low likelihood of singularity. Light Green is failed reachability due to left arm collision with skull. Light Blue is failed reachability due to right arm collision with skull.

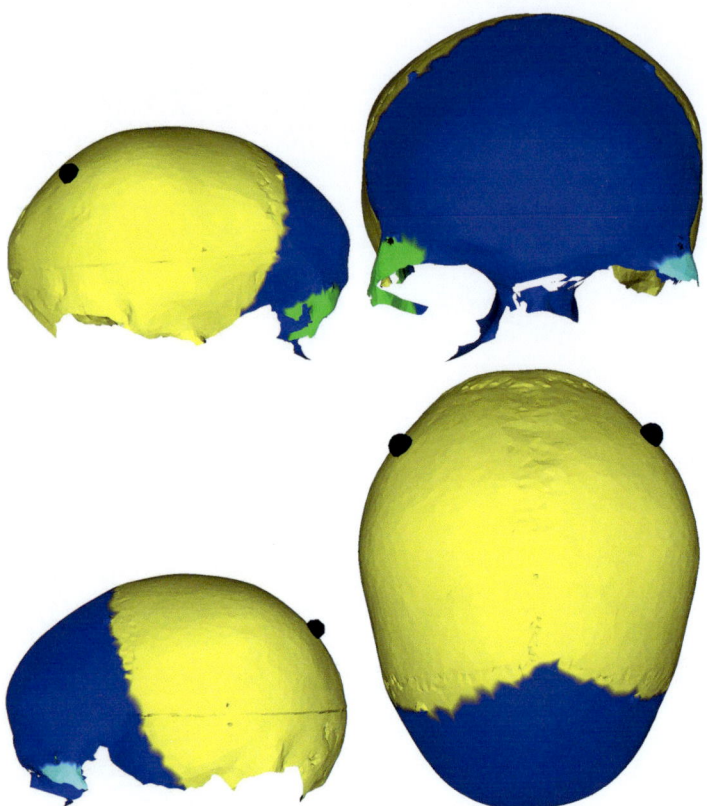

Figure 4.8.: Achievable workspace on skull, with collision analysis for two 100mm curved arms, hinged by spherical joints at anchor points (black). Yellow is reachable, but with high likelihood of singularity problems in control. Dark Blue is reachable and low likelihood of singularity. Light Green is failed reachability due to left arm collision with skull. Light Blue is failed reachability due to right arm collision with skull.

$$[\dot{\Theta}_1\ \dot{\Theta}_2\ \dot{\Theta}_3\ \dot{\Theta}_4\ \dot{\Omega}_5]^T = J^{-1}[\dot{A}\ \dot{B}\ \dot{\Gamma}\ \dot{\phi}\ \dot{\lambda}]^T \qquad (4.7)$$

where $\dot{\Omega}_5$ is the new passive constraint, affecting the third and fourth joints setting up the lean and tilt of the tool, and Γ is the new feedforward term that is a function of the mapping between $[AB]^T$ and $[xyz]^T$.

$$[A\ B\ \Gamma]^T = F([x\ y\ z])^T \qquad (4.8)$$

4.3.7. Error estimation of PKM

While Γ is directly related to the mapping of coordinate systems, and therein the pre-acquired imaging, it is identifiable that it effects the error in the final solution. However, the impact of this error would be limited for the following reason. Errors in Γ would directly effect the rotation of the system around the pivot points. i.e. $\dot{\Omega}_5$. The correlation of this term to the 2D mapped skull surface is limited to a trigonometric relationship with the surface of the skull at the desired point and the error point. It can therefore be predicted that this error is minimal and possibly acceptable should this system to adopted.

The second influence of this error would be in the lean of the tool. The impact of an error in the lean of the tool is seen as negligible in the desired outcome by the surgeons. However, if the pivot point of the tool is a long way above the contact point with the skull, then this angle also carries forward to a greater error in the 2D mapped skull surface. To counter this it would be possible to design the tool holder with a kinematic structure, such that the tilt and lean rotate around a point 0.5mm - 1mm below the surface of the skull. This would require implementation of a remote center of motion kinematic chain. The remote center of motion kinematic chains are normally used in surgical robots as steady hand assistants, for example in the needle placement robot by Boctor et al. [9] or the eye surgery robot by Taylor et al. [123], but the implementation of this concept for error reduction from one kinematic constraint would be new.

The larger, and what is likely to be a more significant error, is a false identification of the pivot points for the robot, and therefore the registration of the image data to the patient data. This is a standard problem for Computer Assisted Surgery (CAS) and has generally been proven to be at an acceptable level. There are two distinctions between this registration and other forms of CAS. Firstly the pivot points here will be used directly in surgery, and not for visual aid of the surgery, and a further registration between the identified points are not required to a world or tracked coordinate system: this is likely to improve our system error by removing one error source; however, secondly we have reduced the number of points to be registered from a typical 4 - 5 to 2. Recalling equation 2.1 this reduction of the N term significantly increases the error. In order to counter this relationship, a possibility exists for implementation of a mechanical solution, whereby the design of the pivot point mounts are enlarged to include 3 or 4 identifiable points each. This solution would increase not only the N terms, but also all three f_k terms, thus greatly increasing the stability of the registration. In all cases mentioned above, it is seen here that the error would be of the same limit as current CAS efforts, and has the possibility of being improved. One disadvantage with such a design however is that the cutting torque would operate directly against the links. This was also highlighted as a design consideration in other works such as by Son et al. [SEKS09].

4.3.8. Swinging Robot Summary

In the above section a possible concept of a Swinging Robot based on a Parallel Kinematic Machine was discussed. After preliminary design analysis, the concept appears possible. Based on this above discussion the challenge here would be to design a machine that meets the following conditions, as well as that of a sterilisable medical solution:

1. No actuator singularities in the workspace (a PKM problem).

2. Well behaved stiffness, though this could be effected slightly by motor torque.

3. Near 100% coverage with curved arms.

4. 4 DOF control on the 5 DOF surface achievable with feed forward term, using pre-surgical imaging data.

5. No requirement for in-surgery calibration or registration of the patient or tools.

4.4. Mobile Robot

The mobile robot is seen to offer the most flexible robotic system; however, it is also the system with the most unknowns. A mobile robot can be attached to any tool, and has an almost unrestricted workspace. Any possible design should not intend on obstructing the handling of the tool, but instead support its movement, similar to a tremor cancelling device. What the mobile robot does require though is a mechanism to achieve grip. On a flat surface such as a building floor where mobile robots often work, this is simply gravity and friction. However, for the required application here, this point here is the most unknown. Friction of wheels moving over bone surface has never been previously studied, and the surface is not flat but spherical, thus gravity cannot be assumed as the method for achieving friction. Numerous forms of control for mobile robots are known; however, their study has normally been limited to elements such as their aforementioned movement over flat surfaces or analysis of kinematics for control of wheels under slippage. No control theory has been developed for non-holonomic movement over a near spherical object.

4.4.1. System Requirements

Mentioned in the previous section, the intent for any mobile robot design would be to support the surgeon in the holding / positioning / tremor cancelling of a tool, in this case a Craniotomy drill piece. To this extent, there are three possibilities for how this design could be pursued. Initially, the concept would be to use a standard Craniotomy drill, with what will be termed as direct handling or alternately indirect handling, and finally with a completely modified, adopted and integrated drill. The concept for the direct handling implies that the surgeon would grip the drill directly, and the mobile robot would be built allowing this handling. The concept for indirect handling implies that the mobile robot would be directly built around the drill, and the surgeon would grip the robot. The final option would be an extension of this design to better integrate the Craniotomy drill into the mobile robot.

The next stage for concept development involved consideration of the wheel configuration. While a standard design for mobile robots involves two driven wheels on a single axis, with a third wheel used for stability positioned forwards, all possible designs were considered. These are shown in Figure 4.9.

Each of the possible designs in Figure 4.9 has advantages and disadvantages. They vary around points such as workspace requirements, stability and required method of control. The concepts start with design A, the most simple and classical of the mobile robots, with unicycle kinematics. This design has both wheels on the same axis and has been the target of a good deal of research. Design B moves to an asymmetric design with the shift of the concept to perform the cutting on the outside of the wheels. This is useful to minimise the amount of workspace required on one side of the trajectory. Design C is an extension of this design to restabilise Design B, with the addition of a small support wheel on the outside of the trajectory. The workspace required for the non-powered support wheel, would be ex-

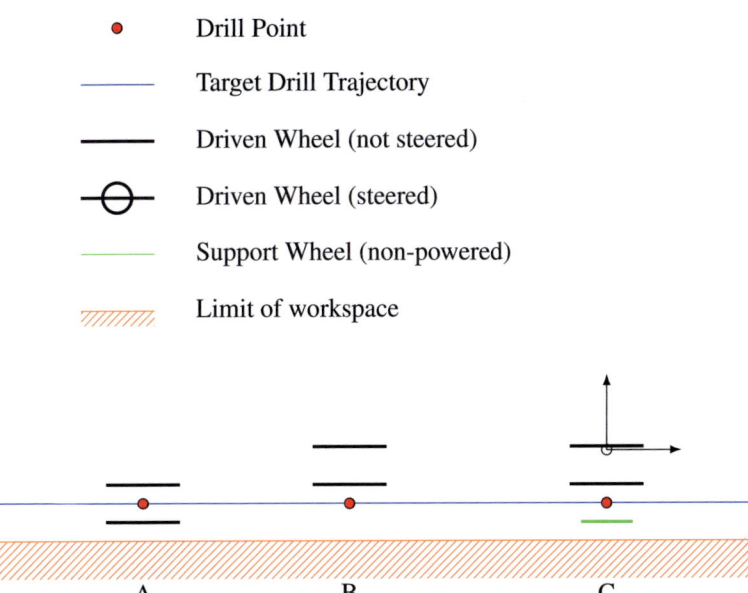

- Drill Point
- Target Drill Trajectory
- Driven Wheel (not steered)
- Driven Wheel (steered)
- Support Wheel (non-powered)
- Limit of workspace

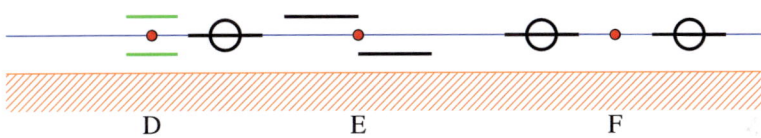

Figure 4.9.: Possible Wheel Configurations

pected to be smaller than that of a normal wheel. Design D starts again with the first design, but replaces the driven wheels with two non-powered support wheels, and includes a single steerable powered wheel. This three wheeled concept increases the stability of the whole design, and by having all driven components relative to a single wheel places them coaxially. This again has the potential to reduce the workspace required for the motors in the area of the skull. Wheel E is an alternate concept of A that moves away from the single axle unicycle kinematics, increasing the stability forwards and backwards, at the expense of an angular tilt. Wheel F extends the possibilities again to a two sttered wheel concept similar, with both wheels in a single line.

4.4.2. Control System Requirements

In all of the above concepts, the mobile robots are shown with two driven components. Either two powered wheels, or a single steered powered wheel. Unlike the previous section on the PKM, a direct correlation cannot be made here between the degrees of freedom to the degrees of control, because the mobile robots do not have a fixed base point, and therefore, almost all control systems are nonholonomic. In this context, the two degrees of control, are able to control 3 degrees of freedom, nominally two components within a coordinate system, and an orientation within that system. i.e. $[AB\phi]^T$ A and B are normally viewed as x and y, but as a similar constraint to that of the PKM analysis, this work does not occur on a flat $[xy]^T$ plane. Therefore it is likely a mapping is required again from the coordinate system $[xyz]^T$. Using the pre-surgical imaging of the patients head, this is again possible.

Within the research of mobile robot kinematics, there is a requirement to define which type of control is required early on, between either a position control, servo control, path following or trajectory tracking. It is clear here that we require more than position control of the robot, but the definitions of servo control, trajectory tracking and path following is often askew. Servo control can be akinned to position control, where the position is moved, as a function of time. Trajectory tracking is the next step where the position as a function of time is pre-planned. Path following is the last possibility, where again the trajectory is planned ahead of time, but the position along that trajectory is not controlled. In analysis of our requirements here, the surgeons had indicated that there was a standard speed at which the cutting should occur at. However, because this speed is not a continuous requirement, and pauses can be made along the trajectory, the approach will be defined as path following with desired velocity.

4.4.3. Mobile Robot Summary

In the above section a possible concept of a mobile robot based that moves directly over the surface of the skull was discussed. After preliminary design analysis, the concept appears possible. Based on this above discussion the challenge here would be to design a machine that meets the following conditions, as well as that of a sterilisable medical solution:

1. Ensure traction between wheels and skull, such that force transfer can be achieved and guaranteed.

2. Minimisation of noise due to hand-held system.

3. Adaption of a 2 DOF control concept to a 3 DOF surface, tracked in 6 DOF.

4.5. Idea Evaluation

The three concepts were evaluated against complexity of design requirements, manufacturability, usability, complexity of control. Design requirements takes into account such items as long thin shafts that still need to be stiff and stable, and the requirement to build a number of active axes into

Table 4.2.: Evaluation of possible robot concepts, each component evaluated from 1 to 3. 1 being extremely difficult to design or not highly beneficial to the user. 3 is the most suitable possible design concept, or a highly beneficial usability.

	Design Req.	Manufac-turability	Control	Usability	**Total**
Mobile Robot	3	2	2	3	**10/12**
Swinging Robot	2	2	1	3	**8/12**
Creeping robot	2	1	2	2	**7/12**

a small area. This complexity of control takes into account such items as likely singularity problems. Manufacturability also included evaluation of such items as required material choice for achieving a sterile solution. The results are shown in Table 4.2.

The Mobile Robot was only slightly forward of the other two ideas. It also fell below the other two in terms of Manufacturability. The main concern here was that any mobile robot needs to have moving axles and linkages that cannot be closed off and sealed, this could lead to a problem with lubrications in a sterile environment. All other designs could have had their linkage sections sealed in silicon or other material above any fixed anchor point with the skull. The decision was made however to proceed with emphasis to be made in the design phase for remedying this point.

5. System Engineering Requirements

Robotic assistant surgical systems are complex systems that involve many interacting components, inclusive of custom hardware and software, sensors, human-machine interfaces and so on. It is essential that for any project involving a large degree of interfaces and generally high technical risk, a systems engineering approach is key to ensuring completion of the project within the scope of both time and money [34]. The Systems Engineering Processes used within the project were based on the ANSI/EIA 632 Processes for Engineering a System standard, as well as the EIA/IS 632 Systems Engineering Standard and in part the MIL-STD-499B Systems Engineering (Draft). The remainder of this chapter describes the outcome of the requirements analysis stage.

5.1. System Need

Central to the engineering design process the need statement was created early and maintained through the design process as:

> Develop for integration into a Surgical Environment a intuitively controlled milling machine for Craniotomies.

5.2. System Design Goals

This project has 3 goals (with traceability to need statement shown through colours):

- Design and build a mobile milling machine.

- System shall be integrated into an Operating Room for use by a Surgeon (not engineer).

- System shall improve on current craniotomy procedures in terms of both safety and accuracy.

5.3. Requirements Analysis

5.3.1. Scope of System

The system shall be established as a standalone system, that can be brought in and out of an Operating Room as required, as per any other tool. For the system to be standalone, is would require development of the following components:

1. A Drive and Gearing subsystem.

2. Robot Structure subsystem.

3. Cabling / connectivity subsystem.

4. Computer subsystem.

5. Auxillary subsystem.

5.3.2. System Boundary

Integration requirements

The system was seen to require integration with the following systems and communications pipes:

1. Patient Data.

   1.1. Pre-operative Imaging.

      1.1.1. DICOM Standard.

   1.2. Planning Trajectory Data.

2. Operating Room Power.

3. Optical Tracking Systems.

4. High Speed Craniotomy Drill. (If not built directly into device).

Notional system integration

While the system integration requirements listed above were determined as necessary for the completion of the system, it was identified that as part of the research project, it was only necessary to demonstrate a tool chain or procedural flow that could achieve the desired result. This was demonstrated with the use of the inhouse developed planning software KASOP. This already included the interface to DICOM data and was capable of developing planning trajectory data. It was therefore now a requirement though to interface with this software completely.

5.3.3. Use Case List

The use case list was defined by the analysis in Chapter 2 in consultation with the medical staff from the Clinic and Policlinic for Maxillo Facial Surgery at the University Hospital of Heidelberg. The end result of the analysis was the main use as that of a Craniotomy for treatment of Craniosynostosis. Where scope in the project allowed, use cases could be extended to other surgical cases where treatment involves a planned craniotomy, such cases include: intra-cranial bleeding, or to allow surgeons access to intracranial tumours, or to allow placement of intracranial probes for the treatment of Parkinsons Disease, or to allow intracranial biopsies to occur.

One exception to the use case list is the craniotomy cut performed through the nose bridge between the eyes. This is removed from the use cases for a number of reasons, the depth of the bone here is considerably greater than any other area of the skull, the closeness to the eyes and optical nerves makes it a sensitive area for the surgeon where exceptional care needs to be applied, and additionally the area is not normally completed with a normal craniotomy, but with a chisel and hammer. Thus it is not possible to be achieved with any robot developed to support a standard craniotomy tool piece.

5.3.4. Functional and Data Requirements

The functional requirements list for the system was developed through use of workflow analysis applied to Functional Flow Block Diagrams (FFBDs), the skull modeling presented later in this chapter and the tradeoff considerations determined between the Technical and Medical requirements. The overall design area space for tradeoffs is shown in Figure 5.1 with two main requirements groups, those being technical, and those being medical. Though there is very strong interdependency between 6 of the tradeoff partners.

The first level requirements developed from the need statement are shown in the following list. These were then allocated to their physical design subsystems from the system scope as shown in Figure 5.2.

Requirements Allocation

   1. Design and build a mobile milling machine for Craniotomy.

      1.1. Machine shall be hand-held.

         1.1.1. Machine shall be < 2kg.

         1.1.2. Machine shall have maximum width of 80mm.

         1.1.3. Machine shall be safe to handle.

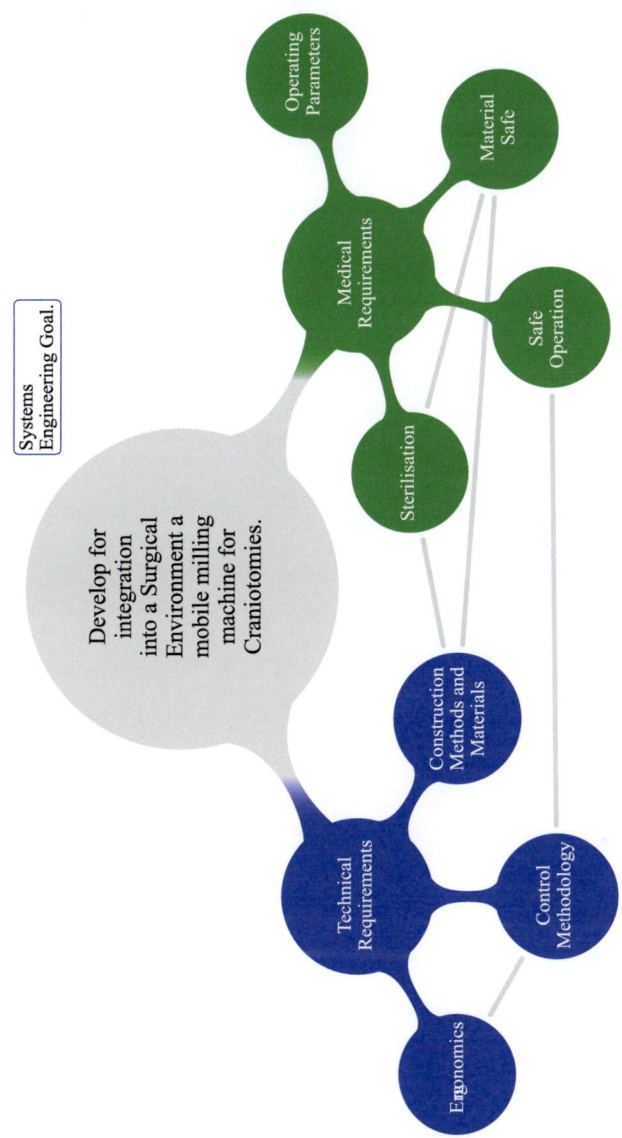

Figure 5.1.: System Engineering Context Diagram, strong interdependency between tradeoff partners is shown by the interconnecting lines.

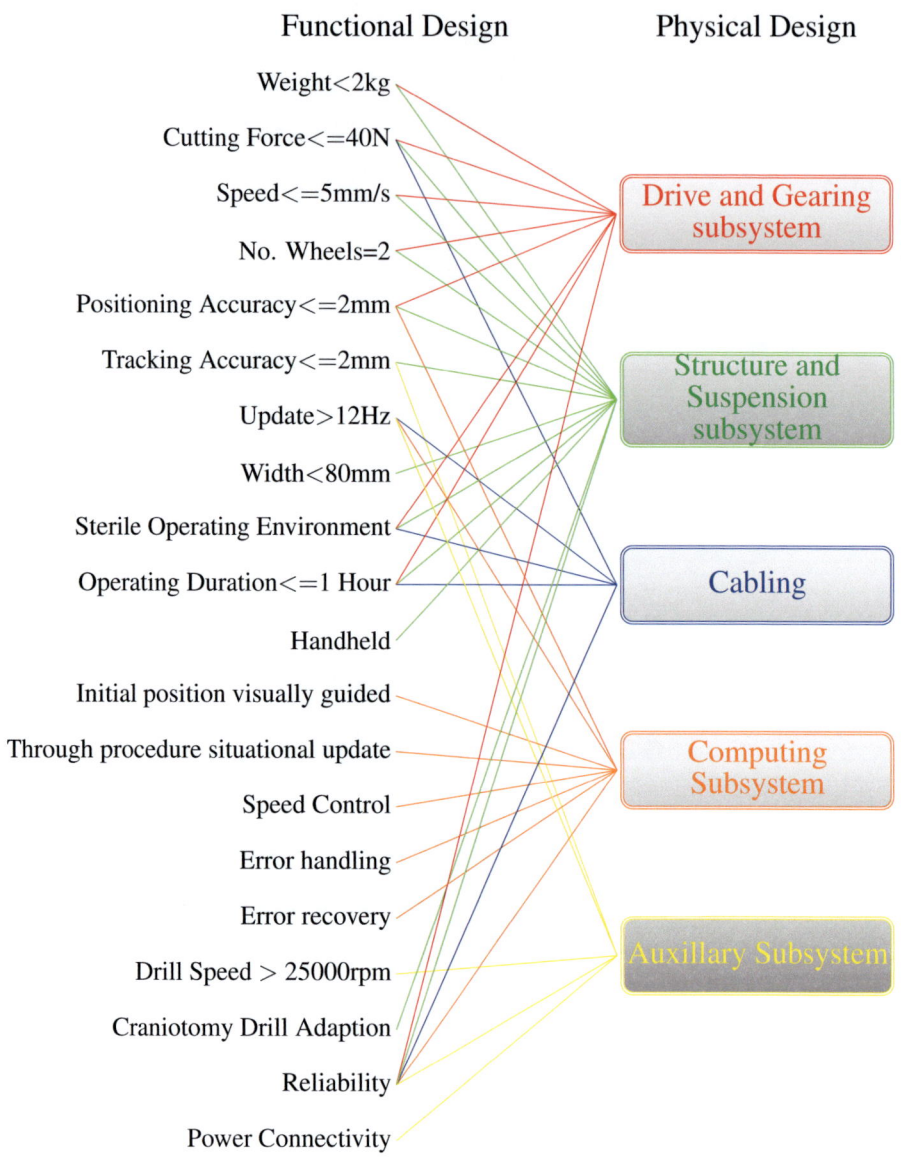

Figure 5.2.: Requirements Allocation

        1.1.3.1. Machine shall not have any open moving features.

        1.1.3.2. Machine shall not exert sudden large forces on surgeons hand.

    1.2. Machine shall be capable of moving over entire skull surface.

2. System shall be integrated into an Operating Room for use by a Surgeon (not engineer).

    2.1. System shall minimise footprint requirements within Operating Room.

    2.2. Milling Machine shall guide surgeons path.

    2.3. Milling Machine able to be sterilised.

    2.4. System shall utilise tracking systems currently available in Operating Room.

    2.5. Surgeon can control robots speed through trajectory.

    2.6. Surgeon can control robots start and stop location.

    2.7. Surgeon to be trained on robot use.

3. System shall improve on current craniotomy procedures in terms of both safety and accuracy.

    3.1. System shall ensure robot can move along trajectory with an overall accuracy of less than ± 2mm (This is based on reported results of previous research projects [7] and [32]).

    3.2. System shall not increase any risk to patient from standard non-robotic procedure.

        3.2.1. System shall not increase duration of procedure.

        3.2.2. System shall not increase invasiveness of procedure.

5.3.5. Reliability Analysis

Through discussion with Doctors (the project clients) the approximate usage of the system was determined for basis of the reliability analysis for the system. The key terms for this usage was seen as the following:

1. 1 - 3 times usage per week.

2. 30 mins - 90 mins operational time per usage.

3. Duty cycle of 5% - 40% operational time per usage.

4. Maximum trajectory length of 40cm per usage.

5. Lifespan of the complete structure 1 - 2 years.

6. Lifespan of drive componentry 4 - 6 months.

7. Desired failure rate < 0.1%.

With these planned terms, the following provided the individual componentry lifecycle definition.

1. MTBF for structure - 1485 hours

2. Complete lifespan for structure - 468 hours

3. MTBF for drive componentry - 1485 hours

4. Complete lifespan for drive componentry - 117 hours

Usage concept for complete system is as follows:

1. Once only storage in 25°C with < 20

2. Local storage in 25°C with < 20

3. Sterilisation of system (less motor and electronic components) in the three phases[2] [1]:

   3.1. Removal of atmospheric air through vacuum pumping

   3.2. Pressurising and de-pressurising (cyclic pressure pumping) of the sterilisation chamber with steam (100% humidity) at 134°C for 3 minutes or 121°C for 15 minutes at up to 100kPa above atmospheric pressure.

   3.3. Drying of the device

4. Attachment of protective wrapping

5. Assembly of drive and electronic componentry

6. Closure of protective wrapping around electronic componentry

7. Calibration of device

8. Local storage in operating room sterile environment up to 2 hours

9. Use of device

10. Replacement of drilling tool

---

[1] The european accepted standard DIN ISO 17665[1] does not specify the exact protocol for Steam Sterilisation and Autoclaving, but instead defines the requirements for the development, validation and routine control of a sterilization process for medical devices. As such, the exact nature and specifics of the process of Steam Sterilisation and Autoclaving varies widely, not only on the procedures of implementing organisations, such as hospitals, but also what the actual devices are capable of achieving. The format for the sterilisation process used above, is determined as one of the more extreme standards that a device may be faced with. Designing our system capable of handling this procedure should then force compliance and mechanical acceptance of the majority of existing procedures. Of note here also, there are additional techniques that can be used for sterilisation, such as Sterilisation with Dry heat, low temperature steam and formaldehyde, or with microbiological methods. Information for the requirements for development of these devices can also be found in the following standards: ISO 20857:2010, ISO 25424:2009 and ISO 11737-2:2009 respectively.

5.3.6. Requirements for the robot - Degrees of Freedom Analysis

From the requirements in Chapter 4 the requirements for all robots were cutting across the surface of the skull. i.e. Drill placement with 2 degrees of freedom (DOF). (Exact nature of coordinate system was yet to be defined, and at this point could be defined as any form of cartesian, spherical, or custom coordinate system). Extending on the placement of the drill with 2 DOF is possible constraint on the depth of cutting. i.e. A third degree of freedom should be either passively allowed, or actively controlled. Finally, the intent to cut a trajectory suggests that the 3 DOF placement is inadequate, and motion defined in a further 2 dimensions is required. i.e. 1 controlled DOF for the drill movement direction vector (in respect to the first two controlled DOF), and a further either passively allowed or actively controlled DOF for allowing or controlling the rate of change of the depth. It is possibly easier to note that we require a near complete system with 5 DOF. The 6th DOF is not lost in the twist of the drill as expected, but actually due to the lack of constraints in the requirement on the angle of the drill. This may seem an overshoot of the requirements analysis, but alternately this was viewed as a freedom in the system. A freedom that also led later to the development of the speed control system. With these thoughts, the dynamics for the robot lie by:

$$v_{robot} = \left(\dot{x}_{surface}, \dot{y}_{surface}, \dot{z}_{surface}, \dot{\theta}_{xy}, \dot{\omega}_z \right) \qquad (5.1)$$

5.4. Requirements from the skull

In order to design any robot, it is essential to have a detailed knowledge of the configuration and working space for the robot. For industrial robotics every work piece handled by the robot is exactly the same. Manufactured to a known precision, the shape and size of the work piece is used to determine the size, type and configuration of the robot(s) that will handle the workpiece. Within medical robotics this is not possible, as every work piece, i.e. each patient, is very different. Therefore, it is necessary to develop a set of likely working spaces for the robot that needs to be designed. It is possible here to develop either a statistical model of the patient, or alternately develop a worst case model from known case studies. For the development of this robot, both methods were required for different workspace components and their associated parameters. This was initially completed in a broad form, to cover any possible robot designs and configurations including fixed hexapods or hinged systems; however, the remainder of chapter will concentrate on the more in depth characteristation of the skull for working space of a mobile robot.

For the wheeled robot there were three key components seen as critical to defining the working space:

- The shape of the skull surface. This is the component that makes up the working space for the robot. The robot must be able to move over the complete surface, within any defined boundary, and without hindrance of any particular surface anomalies.

- The surface of the skull. This is required knowledge for determining that the robot will be able to move without sliding. Or should sliding be permitted, it must be able to occur in a controlled manner. Either sliding or rolling motion, the torques generated by the wheels must be able to convert cutting forces by the Drill.

- The depth material. There are two parts to this section that must be known for the robot design. Firstly the thickness of the bone, and other parameters such as Ash content of the bone can effect the forces required for cutting. Secondly the Dura Matter and other layers underneath the bone can effect the ability of the robot to move freely.

5.5. Parametisation of a likely skull

Many medical textbooks, journals and articles can be found providing an atlas of what a skull should appear like. Figure 5.3 is a typical example from such a medical textbook. We know from the Scientific Grounding, Chapter 2, that we are expecting to operate on a large section of the skull. This is to include the skull sections Os Frontale, Os Parietale, Os Occipitale, Os Temporale and Os Sphenoidale. The majority of the section appears spheroidal, with possible inconsistencies around the Os Sphenoidale and Os Temporale plates, as well as the sutures that join the plates together.

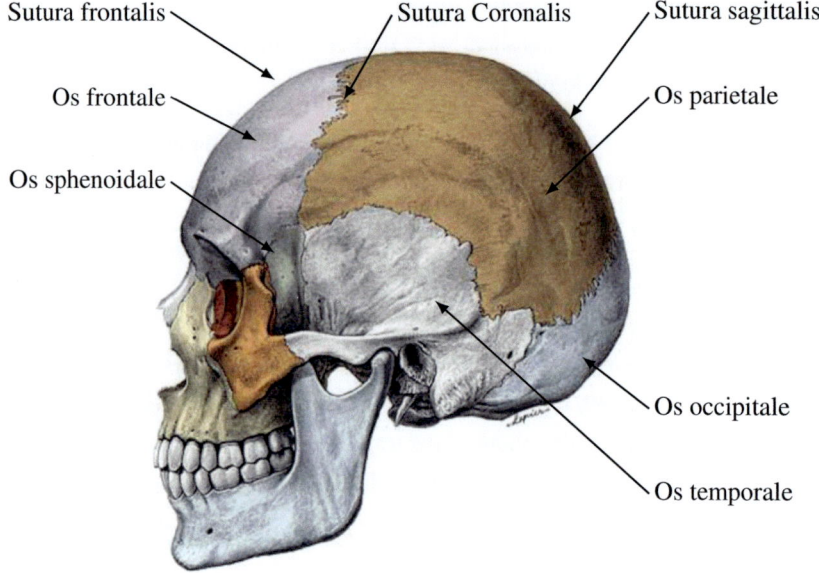

Figure 5.3.: Atlas view of Skull, from Roche

With this concept, there would only be three parameters needed to define the skull. An overall spherical radius r, skull surface discrepancy height b_1 and the maximum slope of any possible discrepancy α. This simplified model is not sufficient because, as discussed earlier in the Scientific

Grounding Chapter 2, the reason for performing these craniotomies, is that the skulls we are operating on are not standard. Therefore, use of a standard template is not an acceptable solution, and the statistical model does not provide any additional information here. As such, it is necessary to develop a more in-depth model, not only of the skull, but of how the robot is expected to travel over the skull while drilling.

5.5.1. Skull Shape Parametisation

In order to further the analysis of the robot moving over the skull, a simplification is made by considering how the robot is likely to move over the skull while performing the craniotomy, and analysis of case studies and how these anomalies could affect the movement. Thus instead of using an atlas or statistical model of the human skull, a conceptual model of the required parameters was defined. Then each parameter was examined individually against the atlas, and a series of case studies of likely patients suffering from Craniosynostosis, to determine the following:

- Is the parameter affected by Craniosynostosis?

- To what extent is the parameter affected by Craniosynostosis?

- Does the extent of parameter change affect the possible movement of the robot?

The first step here is to analyse the skull with a 2D cross section, and thereafter, develop a conceptualised view. Figure 5.4 shows one such view and while the overall structure is complex with many non-linear layers, it is possible however to eliminate several such layers from the analysis that will not affect the design. The remaining layers were then viewed for how they could affect any robot design.

- Skin of Scalp. While the impact of this layer is primarily discounted because it is conceptually removed early in the surgery, it is actually only moved to a different place on the skull. The result for our required conceptualised view is that this new 'skin flap' occupies work space on the site of the craniotomy area. The space occupied by the skin flap is three dimensional (thus in the cross section two dimensional) and can be parametised by the likely distance from the required cut, and the thickness of the skin flap in its new position.

- Periosteum. Similar to the skin of scalp, this layer is removed early in the surgery, and is usually laid onto of the skin fold. Because the thickness of the periosteum is so much smaller than that of the skin, it is possible here in minimising parameters to include the periosteums impact as only a minor increase in the thickness of the skin flap.

- Bone of Skull. The view shown in Figure 5.4 give the indication of two parameters required for characterising the bone, these being the thickness and curvature. However, the skull bone's lower surface is slightly less linear than that shown, and requires two other parameters to describe the maximum deviation in thickness, and the maximum slope of this change.

- Dura Mater. The two layers that make up the Dura Mater, Periosteadl and Meningeal Layers, are seperated from the underside of the skull prior to the craniotomy occuring, but are still in place, and could have an influence on the movement of the craniotomy hook underneath the skull.

The conceptualised 2D cross section, including any possible wheeled robot placement is shown in Figure 5.5.

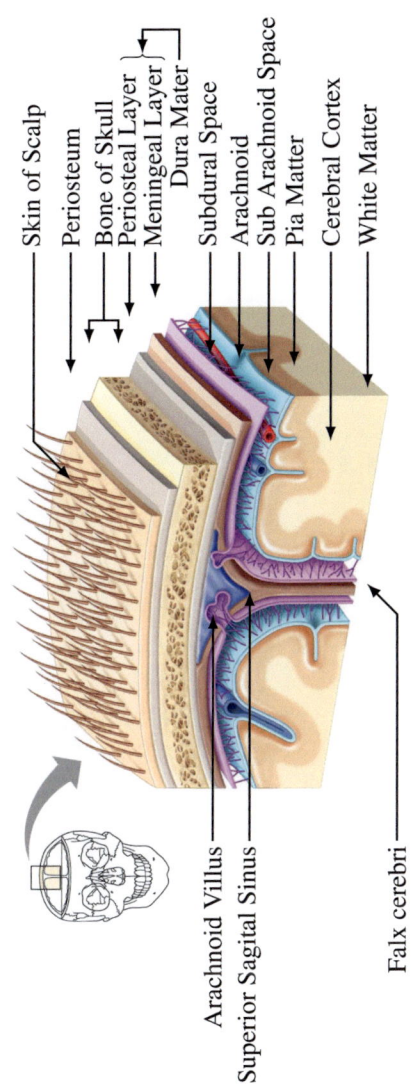

Figure 5.4.: Cross Section through Skull, from Pearson

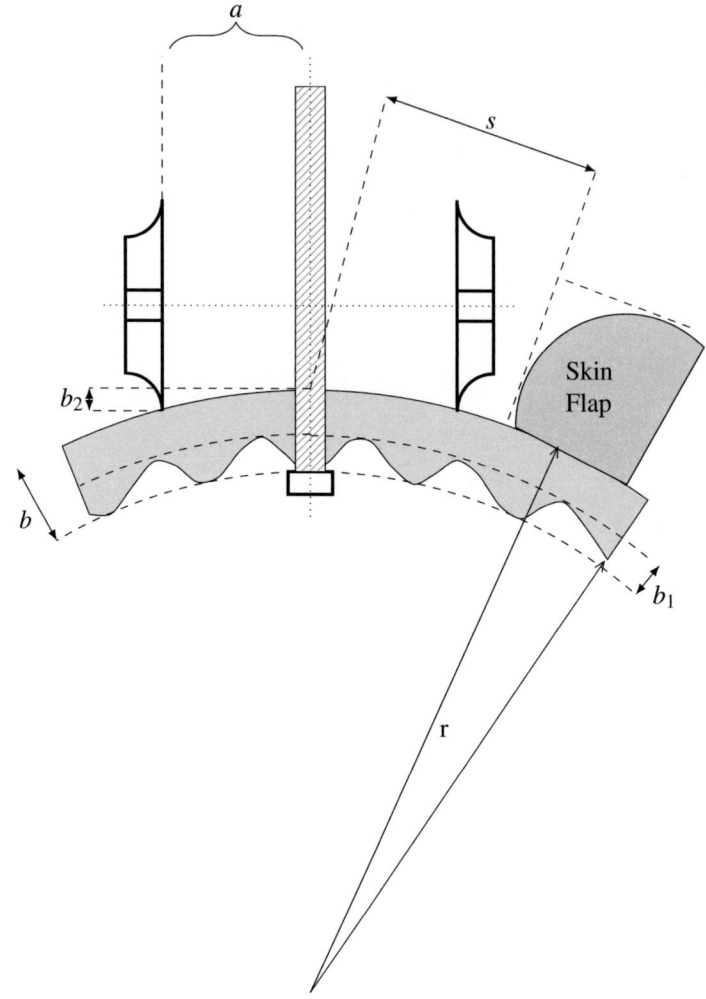

Figure 5.5.: 2D conceptualisation of skull surface parameters

5.5.2. Possible effected parameters

Parameter r

Parameter r is defined as the external surface radius of the skull under the wheel axis. The larger the radius, the flatter and more conventional the surface for the robot. Clearly then of concern for the design, is the possible minimum radius. This can occur in specific cases of Trigonocephaly (metopic synostosis). When this radius gets smaller, the parameter b_3 can be greatly increased.

Parameter b

Parameter b is the maximum thickness of the skull. Combined with r and a it would define the maximum possible cutting depth below the base of the wheels. It can also define the minimum possible cutting depth, a small b combined with a low r can require the cutting tool to raise significantly above the base of the wheels. This parameter is not greatly affected by anomalies, but more based on the age of the patient, and the area on the skull where the craniotomy is occurring. In the portions of the Os frontale directly over the eyes, the thickness of the skull was found to approach 12mm in a number of cases.

Parameter b_1

Parameter b_1 is the maximum deviation from b for the thickness of the skull. In simpler terms, $b - b_1$ defines the minimum thickness of the skull. Again this term can be see that combined with r and a to define the minimum possible cutting depth below the base of the wheels. It can also define the maximum possible cutting depth above the wheels.

Parameter s

Parameter s is the likely distance from a desired craniotomy cut to the skin fold. This parameter is likely to have lead on effects to features such as maximum wheel separation or wheel thickness. Fortunately this parameter is not greatly affected by anomalies. From analysis of various surgeries, it was possible to see that when the skin flap was too close on the skull, it was simply moved further away. This was however not possible in the area over the eyes where the extent it could be moved was greatly limited. This allowed a fixed value to be defined to 20mm. It should also be noted, that from section 5.3.3 an exception was made that the craniotomy would not be performed directly in the area over the eyes where s is at its minimum. It would therefore be possible in design to relax this parameter if required.

5.6. Characterisation of the skulls cutting parameters

There are two primary requirements here for the cutting, these being:

- the speed of the cutting, and

- the force required to push the craniotomy tool tip forward.

These two parameters were provided by the previous work of Bast et al., who performed a study of 11 experienced Neurosurgeons with practical experience of 80-1200 skull operations. From their paper [6], they state that registered forces in cutting had a maxima of 16 N in the feed direction and 21 N normal to the surface; average forces were approximately 1-2 N. A safety factor of 100who looked at the same forces using an ultrasonic chisel. These forces were considerably lower, $< 4N$, providing an alternate tool for possible future integration, though the slow speed of the ultrasonic chisel ($10mm^2min^{-1}$ material removal rate for the chisel, compared with $30 - 60mm^2min^{-1}$ for the conventional tool) could prove prohibitive.

In order to achieve these forces with a mobile robot, it is necessary for the wheels to be able to maintain this level of traction as friction on the surface of the skull. Therefore the next section analyses what is required to achieve this, by study of the skull surface.

5.7. Characterisation of the skull surface

Shown in Figure 5.4 is the typical cross section of the skull. When the craniotomy is performed the upper layers including the Periosteum are already removed, thus the robot sits directly on the top surface of the bone. This outer section of the bone is compound bone (also known as cortical bone or dense bone).

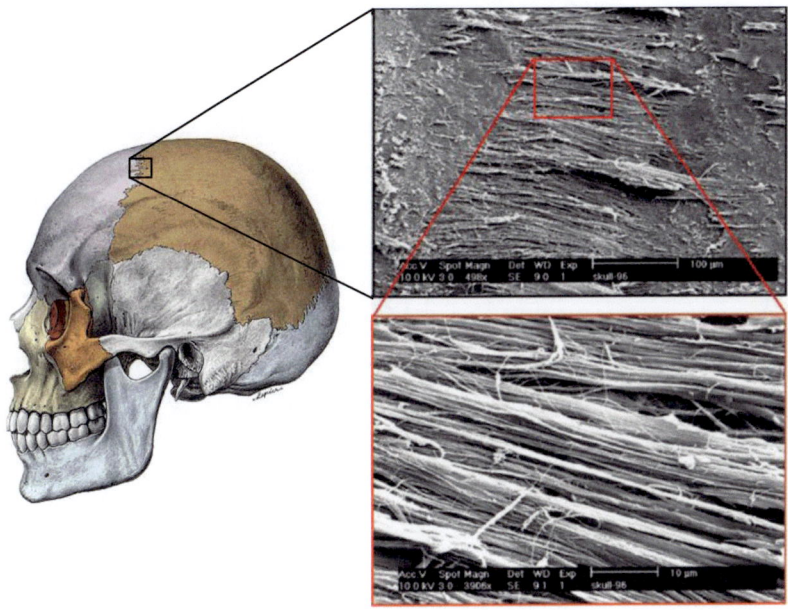

Figure 5.6.: Bone Surface

As a biological material, bone exhibits a complex but heirarchical microstructure and micro components, which results in complex mechanical properties [129]. These properties had been studied by a large number of research team since the 1930s. However, many of these studies were aimed at determining the tensile or ultimate strengths of bone. For example, the importance of tensile loading in the fracture mechanisms of bone was early recognised by Olio et al. in 1937[90], then further studied by Evans in 1957[33] and Currey in 1975[23]. Unfortunately there have been no studies designed to assist in determining friction for movement over the bone surface, and thus required here is a more indepth analysis of the previous results.

The outer layer of bone that predominantly forms the surface of the skull is made of circumferential lamellae. This is a series of fine fibres, $< 1\mu m$ in diametre. Figure 5.6 shows this fine fibres, accentuated at the sutures where they become more pronounced and visible due to their higher growth rate in these areas. There is no research that examines the frictional coefficient of this surface with other materials. Research that examines roughness parameters in relation to bone, is generally concerning bone implant construction, and the holding power of bone. While these studies are typically relevant for the holding strength once bone regrows into the rough surface of an implant, for example [49] , the parameters could be used as guide for designing the wheels. Together with this, it is important to note that the theoretical maximum for any friction, would approach the ultimate tensile stress of human cortical bone. Literature provides many figures for this analysis, but using some of the recent work from Keaveny in [60] , we can approximate the maximum to 65MPa. This figure is taken from the shear ultimate stress, which has a 4.0MPa standard deviation. The first approach to wheel design used this figure to determine the spike's minimum penetration of the skull surface, capable of achieving a surface area of $615nm^2$ against the surrounding bone fibres. Unfortunately this is also highly dependant on the bone fibre direction and force orientation. Additionally, none of this data takes into account the concept to be applied here, i.e. a Surgical application with water spray over the surface. With this information, it was decided to make three possible wheel designs, with varying capabilities and test these empirically.

5.8. Conclusion

This chapter defined the requirements for designing the robot and surrounding control system. The system was to be integrated according to the physical requirements subsystems allocated, and built according to the parameters determined for movement over the skull surface. This was inclusive of all elements for software and hardware necessary to be implemented into the Operating Room environment. The remaining details not known for the wheel design, are discussed later in chapter 7 .

6. Steering Control System

6.1. Current Approach to Mobile Robot Kinematics

Mobile Robots with unicycle kinematics (i.e. dual wheels, single axis) are typically defined in terms of the robots position $\mathscr{P}$ by $[x, y, \phi]$ given with respect to a world coordinate system in 2 dimensions. The orientation defines rotation about an axis normal to the flat surface, and tilt of the robot around the wheel axis is often ignored. While the stability of these robots is often supported by a third or fourth off-axis wheel, exceptions naturally exist.

Kinematics are rarely defined in terms of world coordinates though, and it is necessary to establish a coordinate system with respect to the desired trajectory $\mathscr{T}_d$. An early established method provided by Samson [101] in 1992 was the establishment of a Frenet Frame. The reference trajectory $\mathscr{T}_d$ is given its own reference direction, the orthogonal projection of $\mathscr{P}$ onto $\mathscr{T}_d$ is denoted as $\mathscr{Q}$ and its generalised coordinates are defined as $[x_Q, y_Q, \phi_Q]$. The signed distance error $l(t)$ between $\mathscr{P}(t)$ and $\mathscr{Q}(t)$ is defined as:

$$l(t) = \overrightarrow{\mathbf{N}} \cdot \overrightarrow{Q(t)P(t)}, \tag{6.1}$$

where $\overrightarrow{\mathbf{N}}$ is the unit normal vector of $\mathscr{T}_d$ at $\mathscr{Q}(t)$. $\mathscr{T}_d$ is specified by the initial orientation $\phi_Q(0)$ and the curvature function $\kappa(s(t))$, where $s(t)$ is the signed curvilinear distance from $Q(0)$ to $Q(t)$ on $\mathscr{T}_d$, defined as:

$$s(t) = \int_0^t \overrightarrow{v}_Q(t) \cdot \overrightarrow{\mathbf{T}} dt, \tag{6.2}$$

where $\overrightarrow{v}_Q(t)$ is the velocity vector of $Q(t)$, $\overrightarrow{\mathbf{T}}$ is the unit tangent vector at $Q(t)$ along the reference direction $\mathscr{T}_d$. The orientation error $\tilde{\phi}_Q$ is defined

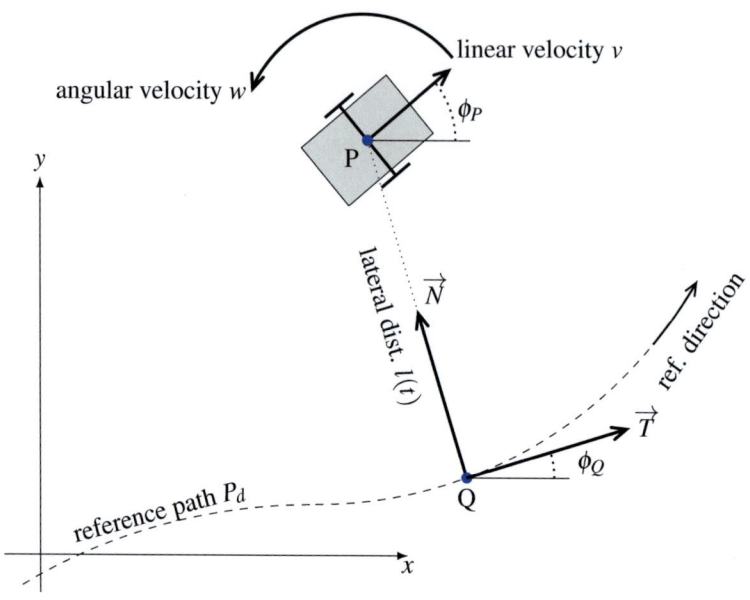

Figure 6.1.: Standard Mobile Robotics Parameters seen in the XY plane, modified from [107]

as $\tilde{\phi}_Q = \phi_P(t) - \phi_Q(t)$. Now, we define new coordinates $(s, l, \tilde{\phi})$ for $\mathscr{P}(t)$ that is defined with respect to Q. This is our new Frenet frame for the rest of this chapter. The rest of section 6.1 includes an extract from the work by Seo et al. and using the approach outlined in the book by Khalil [62] to define the basis for the control theory used in the rest of the chapter from section 6.2. This extract however is critical in understanding the choice of the control system and its proven lemma for establishing a bounded limit to the error. This bounded error being a critical factor in the use of a mobil robot in surgery.

With these new coordinates, a kinematic motion can be described (see [101] for details) as:

$$\dot{s}(t) = \frac{v_P(t)cos\tilde{\phi}(t)}{1 - l(t)\kappa(s(t))}, \tag{6.3}$$

$$\dot{l}(t) = v_P(t)sin\tilde{\phi}(t), \tag{6.4}$$

$$\dot{\phi}(t) = \dot{\phi}_P(t) - \dot{\phi}_Q(t) = w_P(t) - \kappa(s(t))\dot{s}(t), \tag{6.5}$$

where $v_P(t)$ and $w_P(t)$ are linear and angular velocities of $P(t)$ respectively.

With these definitions Seo et al. in [107] define the kinematic path-following problem as:

> Assuming that the angular velocity error $\tilde{w}_P(t) = w_P(t) - w^*(t)$ is bounded by a known constant $\tilde{w}_P$ for all $t \geq 0$, and that $v_P(t) \in [0, v_{max}]$ is Lipschitz continuous for all $t \geq 0$ and does not converge to 0, then find a state feedback controller $w^*(s(t), l(t), \tilde{\phi}(t), v_P(t))$ so that $(l(t), \phi'(t))$ is uniformly bounded for all $t \geq 0$ and ultimately bounded for all $t \geq 0$ with some finite $T \geq 0$.

and using the SMC procedure as given in [62] a control input is defined as:

$$u(t) = w^*(t) - \frac{\kappa(s(t))v_P(t)cos\tilde{\phi}(t)}{1 - l(t)\kappa(s(t))}, \tag{6.6}$$

simplifying 6.5 to:

$$\begin{aligned}
\dot{\tilde{\phi}}(t) &= w_P(t) - \frac{\kappa(s(t))v_P(t)cos\tilde{\phi}(t)}{1 - l(t)\kappa(s(t))} \\
&= u(t) - \tilde{w}_P(t).
\end{aligned} \tag{6.7}$$

Importantly for the derivation of the control input to meet the bounded error constraints, Samson et al. proposes and proves in [107] a lemma for an SMC according to the formulation in [62] as the following:

Lemma 6.1.1. *Convergence of z(t). A SMC u(t) is proposed according to [62] as follows:*

$$u(t) = -\frac{kv_P(t)sin\tilde{\phi}(t)}{1+k(l(t))^2} - (\bar{w}_P + b_1)sat\left(\frac{z(t)}{\varepsilon}\right). \tag{6.8}$$

where b_1 is a positive constant, $\bar{w}_P$ is the known upper bound of $|\tilde{w}_P(t)|$, ε is chosen to satisfy:

$$0 < \varepsilon < Tan^{-1}(kL) \tag{6.9}$$

and sat($\cdot$) is defined as

$$sat(y) = \begin{cases} y, & if\ |y| < 1 \\ sqn(y), & if\ |y| \geq 1 \end{cases} \tag{6.10}$$

Here it is more useful to rewrite the SMC input u(t) in terms of the desired rotational velocity $w^*(l(t), \tilde{\phi}(t), v_P(t))$ as:

$$
\begin{aligned}
w^*(l(t), \tilde{\phi}(t), v_P(t)) &= \frac{v_P(t)cos\tilde{\phi}(t)}{1-l(t)} - \frac{kv_P(t)sin\tilde{\phi}(t)}{1+(kl(t))^2} \\
&\quad - (b_1)sat\left(\frac{z(t)}{\varepsilon}\right)
\end{aligned}
\tag{6.11}
$$

When this controller is applied to the mobile robot system, the sliding mode error z(t) becomes strictly decreasing and eventually reaches $|z(t)| \leq (\varepsilon)$ in finite time and remains in there thereafter.

With this lemma proven, a theorem based on this information is derived by Seo et al.:

Theorem 6.1.2. *For all* $(l(t), \phi'(0)) \in W$, *if the control input in 6.8 is used,*
then, $(l(t), \phi'(t))$ *is bounded in the positively invariant set W for all* $t \geq 0$
and is ultimately bounded in the positively invariant set $W_{\varepsilon, \delta} \subset W$.

The proof to 6.1.2 provided by Seo et al. provides the required information to ensure the safe operation of the surgical robot in this project. Once $(l(0), \phi'(0)) \in W$, the trajectory $(l(t), \phi'(t))$ never escapes W
and D. However, if $(l(0), \phi'(0)) \in D - W$, then it can be $|l(0)| \leq L$, but
$|\phi'(0) + Tan^{-1}(kl(0))| > Tan^{-1}(kL)$, and the robot can escape D at certain
time. This case can be resolved easily if the robot is initially at rest. In
this case, prior to any forward move, we rotate the robot around its centre
and increase or decrease $\phi'(t)$ until $(l(t), \phi'(t))$ reaches W. Through this
preliminary step, we can make $(l(t), \phi'(t))$ stay in D for all $t \geq 0$ and
$(l(0), \phi'(0)) \in D$. Interpreting in terms of the sliding mode error $z(t)$ until
it reaches $|z(t)| \leq Tan^{-1}(kL)$. This rotation is realized by applying the pro-
posed controller 6.11 while keeping $v_P(t)$ to zero. We keep $v_P(t)$ by setting
$v^*(t)$ to zero, where $v^*(t)$ denotes the speed command or the desired value
of $v_P(t)$.

6.2. Approach Definition and Modification to 3D

For the robot in this paper, the use of 2D kinematics, is unfortunately too
limited without modification. A skull's surface is 3D and predominantly
non-linear. This means that the simple adoption to a spherical coordinate
system is too limited. Additionally in this project all parameters, including
such aspects as robot tilt, need to be determined without knowledge of the
target surface. Instead the following problem description is used.

The robot is modeled with the two wheels on a single axis moving on an
arbitrary surface. In this architecture, the two identical wheels of radius r
are mounted collinearly at a distance b and the robots position $\mathscr{P}$ is defined
as the center of wheel axis. $\mathscr{P}$ needs to be defined by both position and
orientation.

The aim of this project is however not the tracking of point $\mathscr{P}$ but instead the drilling axis which performs the craniotomy cut. The high speed drill performing this cut, is positioned several millimetres forward of $\mathscr{P}$ (at a distance c). The high speed drill can move along its own cutting axis, with the intent that it's tip tracks the bottom of the skull.

The cutting axis $\overrightarrow{\mathscr{C}_{\mathscr{A}}}$ is defined by two points, $\mathscr{C}_{\mathscr{T}}$ (Tip of the drill) and $\mathscr{C}_{\mathscr{V}}$ (Top of the drill). The forward direction of the robot is defined with a point $\mathscr{F}$ positioned forward of $\mathscr{C}_{\mathscr{T}}$. i.e with the vector $\overrightarrow{\mathscr{C}_{\mathscr{T}}\mathscr{F}}$.

The trajectory function for path following was defined as the series of points $T_i(x,y,z), i \in \{1..N\}$ where $N \in \mathbb{Z}$ is the number of points in the trajectory.

6.2.1. Lateral Offset

As with the 2D kinematics described above, it is necessary to determine the lateral offset $l(t)$ of the robot from the trajectory, and the angular error $\tilde{\phi}(t)$ between the robots heading and the desired trajectory. As the surface is unknown, the contact point of the drill with the skull is ignored. More directly the error distance $l(t)$ is determined by finding the minimum distance between the segments $\overrightarrow{\mathscr{C}_A}$ and $\overrightarrow{T_i T_{i+1}}$. (Here only the drill length segments may be used and not the complete vector projections. This is necessary to prevent false minimums occurring due to the cutting axis $\overrightarrow{\mathscr{C}_A}$ projecting from one side of the skull to the other side of the skull where another part of the trajectory may lie.) Similarly the trajectory segment $\overrightarrow{T_i T_{i+1}}$ must be used in order to prevent false minimums on concave shaped trajectories. The trajectory pair found at the minimum is labeled as $\overrightarrow{T_m T_{m+1}}$ The point on $\overrightarrow{\mathscr{C}_A}$ where this minimum occurs is approximated to be where the intersection with the skull occurs, noted as $\mathscr{I}$.

Figure 6.2.: Problem Definition for Craniotomy Cutting Robot, with exaggerated wheel offset b for clarity. This conceptualised view of the robot is taken from the Blender Simulation used in the control theory development. The robot is shown with only its four key elements as used in the bullet physics simulation, the two wheels, the cutting tip of the craniotomy, and a conceptualised point P around which the robot rotated. The trajectory points $T_i(x, y, z)$ are shown as spherical markers on the surface of the skull.

91

6.2.2. Angular Error

The angular error $\tilde{\phi}(t)$, as with the 2D kinematics derivation, is defined as the angular error in the direction of motion. The angle between $\overrightarrow{T_m T_{m+1}}$ and $\overrightarrow{C_T F}$ includes components of tilt from the robot and cannot be used. As an example, it can be seen that the robot can drive forward almost completely leaned over. Here $\overrightarrow{C_T F}$ would point directly into the skull, and the angle between $\overrightarrow{T_m T_{m+1}}$ and $\overrightarrow{C_T F}$ would be $\approx 90°$.

In order to remove the tilt component of the robot, two planes are defined. The first plane Π_1 for the robot is defined through points $\mathscr{F}$, $\mathscr{C}_\gamma$ and $\mathscr{C}_\mathscr{J}$. i.e. with a normal along the wheel axis, and independent of any tilt. The second plane Π_2 is defined by two vectors: the cutting axis, $\overrightarrow{\mathscr{C}_\mathscr{J} \mathscr{C}_\gamma}$ and the closest trajectory segment $\overrightarrow{T_m T_{m+1}}$. The angular difference between these two planes is used as the angular error $\tilde{\phi}(t) = cos^{-1}(\hat{n}_1 \cdot \hat{n}_2)$. This approach removes any error due to surface irregularities from height changes or roll of the robot from side to side (i.e. outside the plane Π_1).

6.2.3. Desired Velocity

In accordance with the initial intent for an intuitive control system, it was necessary to achieve a speed control by interpreting a native action of the surgeon.

The solution shown in Figure 6.5 was implemented using a weighted multiplication of three inputs. Two inputs come from an interface box we developed for the Aesculap High Speed Drill controller. From this box we determine firstly whether or not the surgeon wants the robot to do anything. i.e. A binary gated switch based on the foot pedal that controls the drill. Secondly we extract the torque of the drill motor. By knowing if the drill is having difficulty cutting, we decrease the forward speed, allowing longer time cutting. This decreases the forces on the wheels, and helps in maintaining traction.

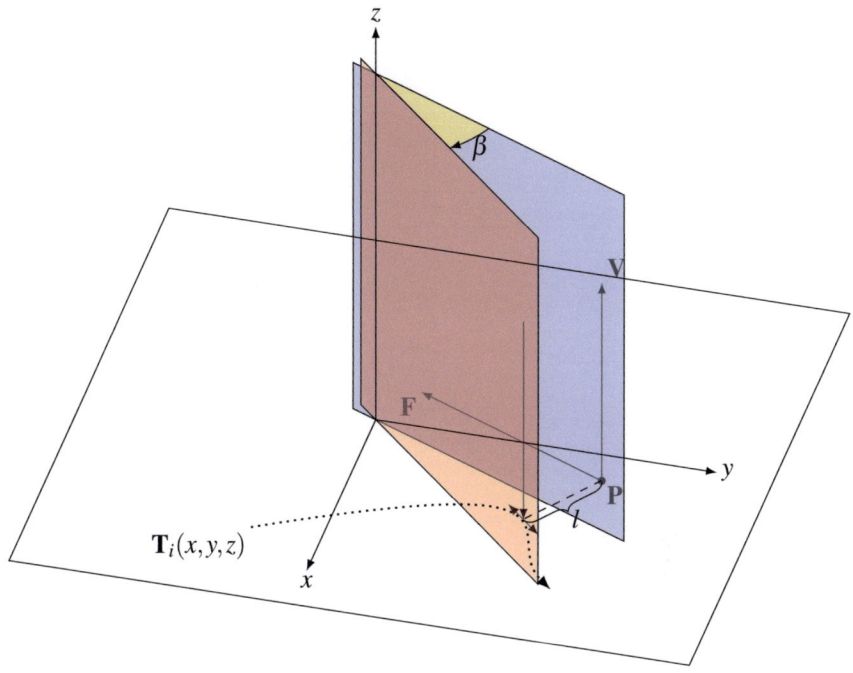

Figure 6.3.: The planes used to determine the lateral error and Angular Error for the Steering control.

As mentioned above for the shared control theory, the intent however comes mainly from a third input from the optical tracking. That being the tilt of the robot β around its wheel axis. We take $\beta = 0$ as the normal from the trajectory. This normal is defined from a third plane defined by two vectors, one taken as the cross product between the closest line between $\overrightarrow{T_m T_{m+1}}$ and $\overrightarrow{\mathscr{C}_{\mathscr{T}}\mathscr{C}_{\mathscr{V}}}$, and the second vector $\overrightarrow{T_m T_{m+1}}$. i.e. The normal to Π_3 is $\hat{n}_3 : (\overrightarrow{T_m T_{m+1}} \times \overrightarrow{\mathscr{C}_{\mathscr{T}}\mathscr{C}_{\mathscr{V}}}) \times \overrightarrow{T_m T_{m+1}}$

6.2.4. Angular Steering Control

Using $l(t)$, $\tilde{\phi}(t)$ and $v_P(t)$ from above an approach similar to that of [107] with details in [101] is used to determine the kinematic motion of the robot.

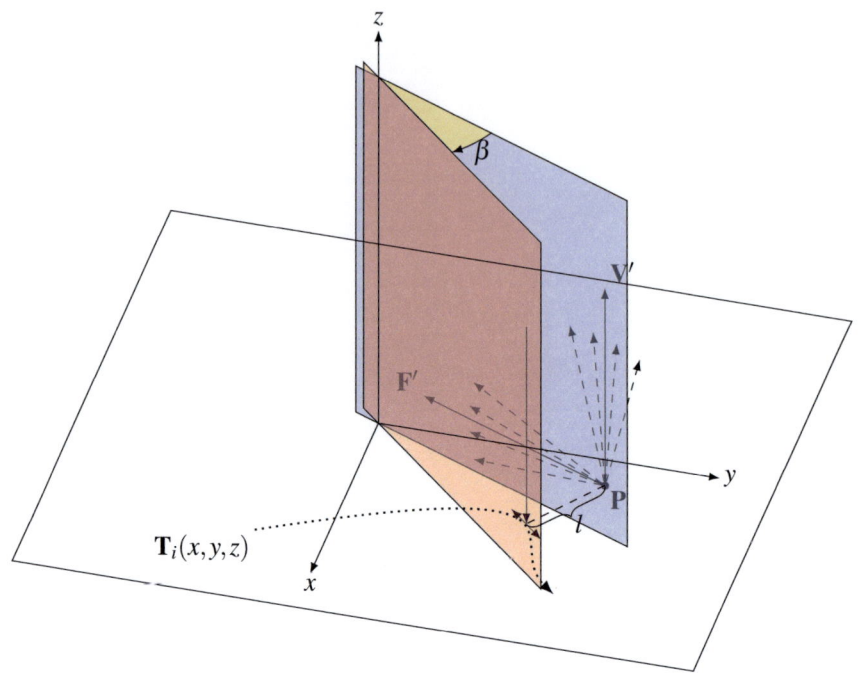

Figure 6.4.: Multiple Tilt

A modified function for the desired angular velocity control signal $w(t)^*$ from [107] is shown in eq 6.11.

$w(t)^*$ is the desired rotational velocity in rad/s around the drill axis. k, b_1 and ε are gain factors that determine the desired approach angle to the trajectory. $sat()$ is a saturation function between -1 and 1. $z(t)$ is a sliding mode control function allowing the setting of a safety margin around the trajectory. The original function also included a $K(s(t))$ curvature function to accomodate for turns in the trajectory. This was removed because the trajectory here uses segments defined with sub-millimetre lengths, and the curvature between any two segments is very limited.

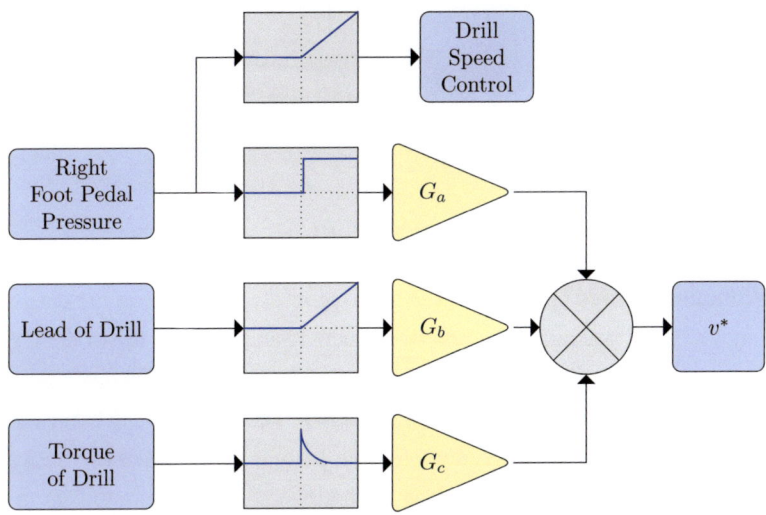

Figure 6.5.: Speed control determination for Robot

6.2.5. Wheel velocities

In order to convert this rotational velocity into wheel velocities, it needs to be shifted to the rotation around $\mathscr{P}$, the centre of the wheel axis. While the distance between the drill axis and $\mathscr{P}$ is a set distance, a direct shift cannot be employed. The problem is that due to the tilt of the robot, the drill axis can penetrate the skull forward or behind the centre of the wheels. This can lead to a complete reversal of the intended rotational velocity. Thus, an approximate position of the drill axis to skull penetration is determined, and a modified translation distance determined that takes the tilt into effect.

$$c_m = \frac{c - r\sin(\beta)}{\cos(\beta)} \tag{6.12}$$

The wheel velocities are then determined.

$$v_R = sgn(c_m)w^*\sqrt{b^2 + c_m^2} + v_P$$

$$v_L = -sgn(c_m)w^*\sqrt{b^2 + c_m^2} + v_P \tag{6.13}$$

6.3. Optical Tracking Implementation

Within the desired application, the tracking of the robot and of the desired trajectory, are performed by optical markers residing on the top of the high speed drill, and on the head of the patient. The offsets of $\mathscr{C}_\mathscr{Y}$ and $\mathscr{C}_\mathscr{I}$ are determined through a process of pivotisation. This involves the movement of a pointer about the desired point. The pointer has a separately tracked marker set at its end. The tracking of the marker set will extrapolate to a sphere. The centre of which is the point about which the item was moved. $\mathscr{F}$ is a virtual point that sits forward of the robot in the direction of movement. Here the robot is placed in a small jig that provides support against tilting (similar to providing training wheels forward and backwards), and driven forwards with equal wheel velocities. To remove any offset due to poor alignment of the training wheels, $\mathscr{F}$ is shifted in the z vector into the xy plane of $\mathscr{C}_\mathscr{I}$. The length of $\overrightarrow{\mathscr{F}\mathscr{C}_\mathscr{I}}$ is given unit length.

The position of the trajectory with respect to the marker body on the skull is determined through a rigid body registration, using the optical pointer pivotised on at least 3 titanium screws inserted into the skull, prior to surgery, and whose positions are known during the surgical planning.

In order to determine the robot position relative to the trajectory, it is necessary to translate the three positions $\mathscr{C}_\mathscr{Y}$, $\mathscr{C}_\mathscr{I}$ and $\mathscr{F}$ into the patient coordinate system. This involves firstly getting the two tracked frames of the robot M_R and the patients rigid body M_P from the optical tracking system. The three points of the robot are found in the world coordinate system by multiplication of their offsets determined in calibration as per equation 6.14. The offsets were determined during calibration, see section 9.3.1 for more information. These positions are then transformed into the patient co-ordinate system by multiplying their offset from the rigid body position, by the rigid body frame, equation 6.15 Using the by $\mathscr{H}_{RT}$. Using the transla-tions from robot positions to robot marker as $\mathscr{H}_{\mathcal{C}_V \mathcal{M}_\mathcal{R}}$, the robot marker to patient marker as $\mathscr{H}_{\mathcal{M}_\mathcal{R} \mathcal{M}_\mathcal{P}}$ and the translation from patient marker to tra-jectory as $\mathscr{H}_{\mathcal{M}_\mathcal{P} \mathcal{T}}$. These frames and translations are shown in Figure 6.6. In the trajectory coordinate system the robot positions are noted as (similar equations for $\mathcal{C}_\mathcal{T}'$ and $\mathcal{F}'$):

$$C_V' = M_R * C_V^*$$
$$C_T' = M_R * C_T^*$$
$$F' = M_R * F^* \tag{6.14}$$

$$C_V^P = (C_V' - M_{P(Trans)}) * M_P$$
$$C_T^P = (C_V' - M_{P(Trans)}) * M_P$$
$$F^P = (F' - M_{P(Trans)}) * M_P \tag{6.15}$$

$$\mathcal{C}_V' = \mathcal{C}_V \times \mathscr{H}_{\mathcal{C}_V \mathcal{M}_\mathcal{R}} \times \mathscr{H}_{\mathcal{M}_\mathcal{R} \mathcal{M}_\mathcal{P}} \times \mathscr{H}_{\mathcal{M}_\mathcal{P} \mathcal{T}} \tag{6.16}$$

6.3.1. Optical Tracking Calibration

A key component to the successful operation of the control system is the calibration of the coordinate systems. Without this calibration, the control systems calculations are not able to accurately determine the correct path for the robot, and hence the corresponding wheel velocities determined are non-sensical. On the second point, without a determination of the coordin-ate systems, it is not possible to determine when the robot is being tilted by the surgeon, and no realistic control interface method can be achieved. With respect to Equation 6.16, there are two key transformation terms that need to be determined and calculated, $\mathcal{H}_{\mathcal{M_P} \mathcal{T}}$ (patient to world coordinates) and $\mathcal{H}_{\mathcal{C_Y} \mathcal{M_R}}$ (robot to world coordinates). This is discussed later in the Surgeon Robot interaction chapter as part of the workflow integration. See section 9.3.1.

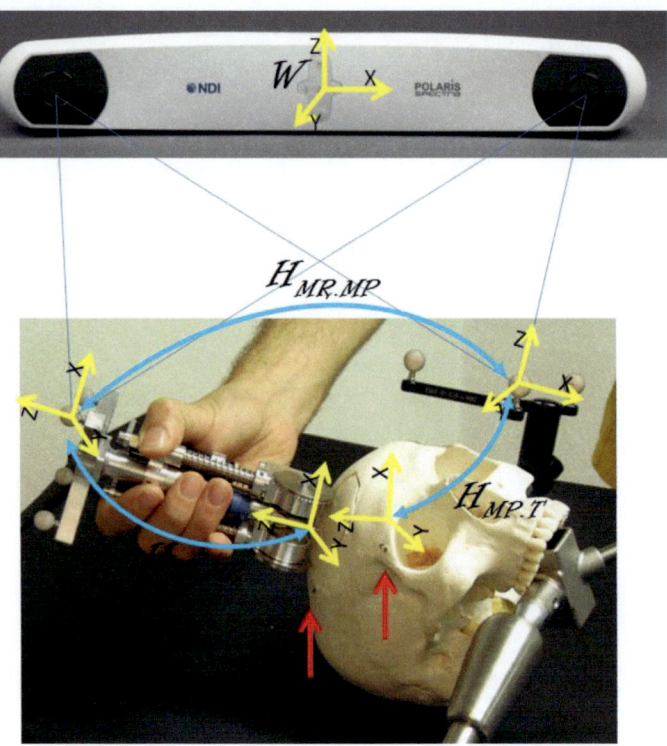

Figure 6.6.: Frame Determination and transformations shown for relevant bodies with IR reflecting optical tracking markers. (An earlier prototype of the robot is shown) The red arrows indicate the titanium skull markers used for pivotising the skull for registration.

7. Mechatronic Design

With selection of the drive concept in chapter 4, the following chapter outines the final realization of the wheel drive, and the implementation of the borer depth and angle control mechanisms. This chapter deals with the principle modeling variants, and the calculations based on the systems specifications finalised in chapter 5. This final design, with the major components indicated, is shown in Figure 7.1.

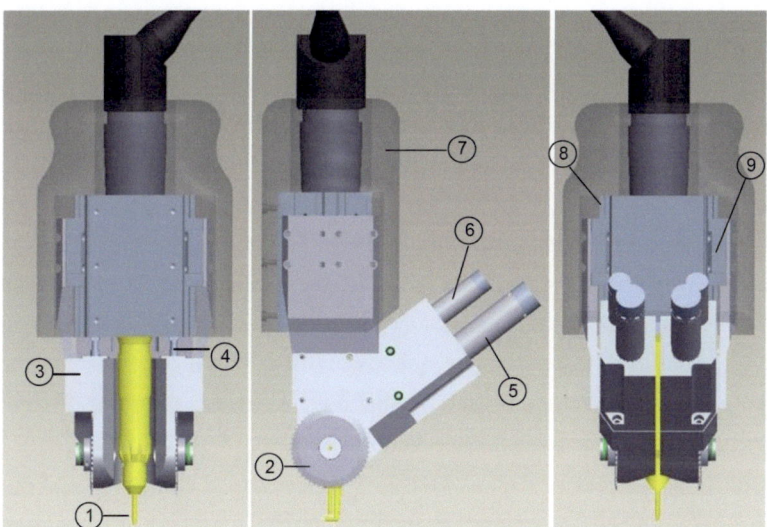

Figure 7.1.: Left: Front view, Middle: Side view, Right: Back view of the CAD construction of the Craniostar Design. The parts can be seen as: 1. Craniotomy Drill, 2. Wheels, 3. Lower Structure, 4. Vertical Spindle, 5. Drive Motors, 6. Vertical Spindle Motors, 7. Handgrip, 8. Vertical Slide Guides, 9. Vertical Sliders.

7.1. Principle Modeling

After brainstorming the drive concepts from Section 4.4, two main drive realizations were found that could allow the wheel control for forwards and backwards, and simultaneously the control of the drilling depth and angle. The combination between these two drive concepts is very tightly bound, and it was known early that the selection of mechanical linkage would greatly affect the accuracy and complexity of control needed to achieve independent control. This linkage is shown briefly in Figure 7.2.

7.1.1. Principle Modeling for Drive Train

For the principle modeling was the drive train of the robot fundamentally modeled for achieving the trajectory control. These possibilities were then investigated as integration with the craniotomy cutting control, i.e. to set the depth and angle of cutting. i.e. the left side of Figure 7.2 were investigated at how two separate drive components could be dislocated from each other, with the possible linkages on the right side of the Figure. Two of these first concepts from the left side of Figure 7.2 are then shown in Figure 7.3.

The implications of the drive linkage selection impacts the overall design in two very specific ways, namely for the sterilisabiliity of the system and for the requirements of the trajectory control. The sterilisability of the system, as outlined in the systems requirements chapter, is highly reliant on the selection of the motors, or their adaptability. There are a number of commercially available autoclavable motors; however, these are quite limited with respect to extras such as encoders. The sensitive electronics and optics in the encoders are generally the limiting factor, and it was recognised early in the project that such trajectory control, requiring velocity control on the motors, could only be achieved with encoder embedded motors. For the solution there had to be another method. Other research groups had created custom encoders that could be attached to the motor shaft, but at a significant distance from the motors. Essentially unsterilised, they were

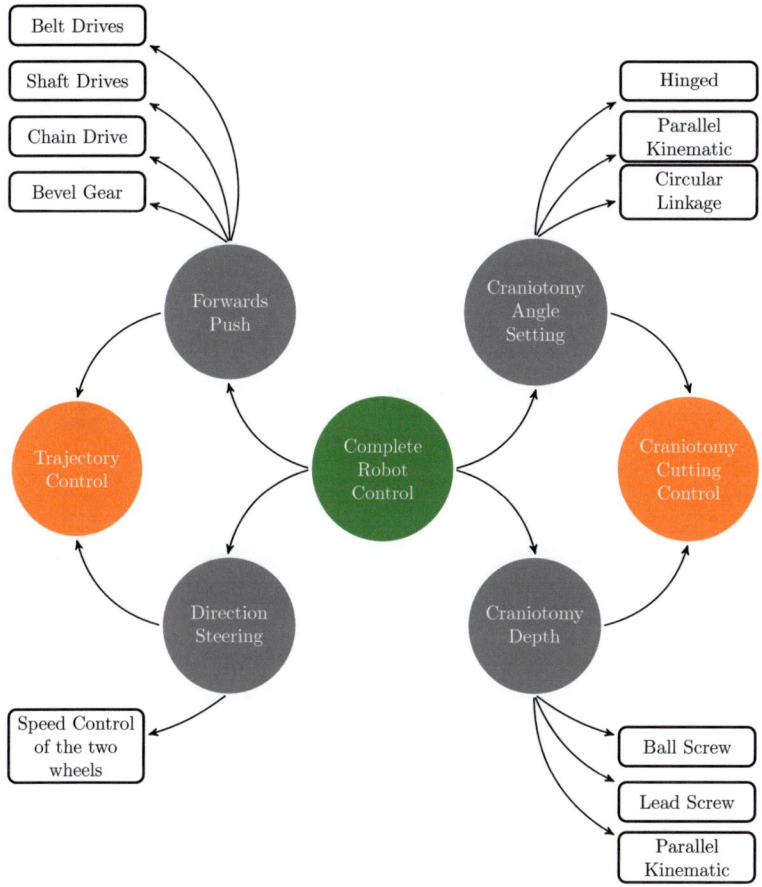

Figure 7.2.: Possible Mechanical Construction Options

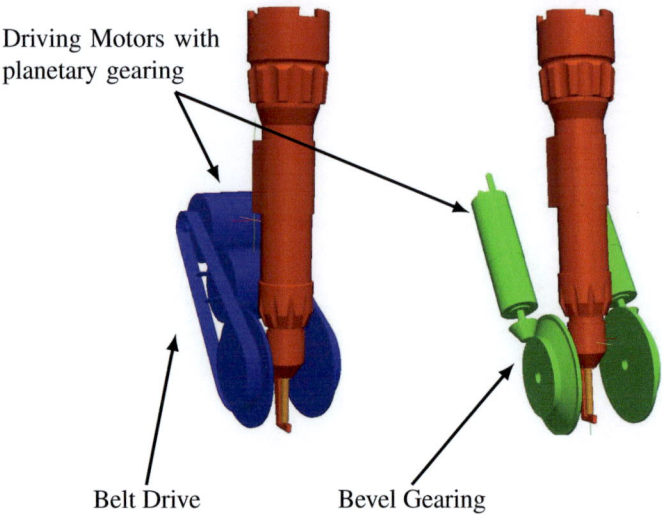

Driving Motors with planetary gearing

Belt Drive   Bevel Gearing

Figure 7.3.: Two possible mechanical drive options, left is the belt drive with short horizontal set motors, right is the bevel geared drive with longer thinner motors.

wrapped in sterilised cloth after attachment to the motor before the start of the surgery. However, this setup leads to a number of problems for the handheld tool that we are trying to design. Firstly the long extension of the motor shafts, leads to uneasy handling for the surgeon and secondly, long shafts for precision encoders do not equate to an overly accurate system. Long shafts have a large moment of inertia, they can twist very slightly, impeding the position reporting, and also increase the strain on the motors, that are to be as small and light as possible for the surgeon to lift.

An alternate system investigated was the incorporation of sealed, though non-sterile motors after the sterilization of the robot. The enclosure of the motors could be made of a simple shape allowing wrapping in surgical cloth, and with appropriate additions for a connections mechanism. This requirement for a connections mechanism led the design process away from that of the belt drives. For an implementation where the motors would need to be connected from opposing sides, and Alternately, the bevel geared design, could have both motors in parallel, allowing a shaft connection system to be relatively simple to implement.

7.1.2. Principle Modeling for Cutting System

The second issue here mentioned is the selection of drive concept for the craniotomy drill and depth angle. Figure 7.4 shows the two main linkage choices. On the left is a parallel kinematic option, and on the right a hinged design. It can be seen that the design on the right suffers greatly in the dependency of one system on the other. The system on the left, the parallel kinematic, shows a completely independent operation of the two systems. With the parallel kinematic option the depth of the cut is regulated by the linear adjustment of each wheels axle in comparison to each other. If the wheel axles are moved simultaneously and at the same velocity, the cutting depth can be varied. If the axles are moved independently of one another, the angle of the cut can be varied. The parallel kinematic also allows the two motions to be combined. One disadvantage of this system, is that when the cutting occurs at an angle, the wheels are also tilted from the surface normal. This could lead to complications in maintaining the required traction. The linked kinematic offers a more separated control of the two movements. The linkage is for the control of the cutting angle, and another linear drive is required for the cutting depth.

Another advantage of the parallel kinematic is the possibility to place the motors for this linkage in the same section as that as the drive motors. This leads to the later discussed element of the shaft connectors and sterilisability. This can only be achieved though if all motor axes are parallel, and this is seen in the modeling of the two systems shown in Figure 7.4. For this to be achieved, it does require that the depth / angle motors are connected to their linear guides through another bevel gear. All the advantages

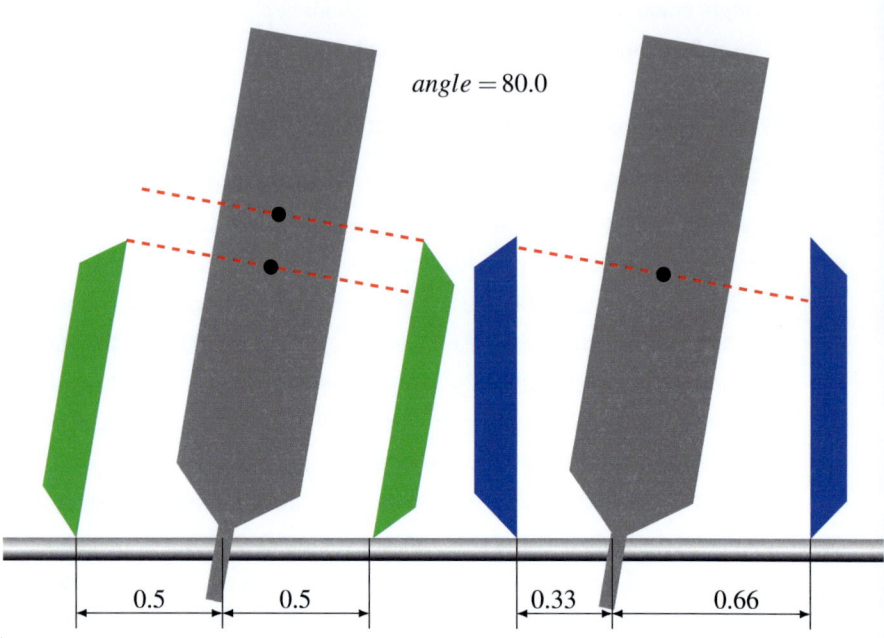

Figure 7.4.: Example effect of linkage choice on position of drill vs angle of craniotomy, left picture shows the parallel kinematic setup, through either
ball screws or lead screws, right picture shows a single hinged linkage
for the craniotomy.

of the parallel kinematic option compared with the linked concept fixed the design on this concept.

A side view of this final concept, with bevel gear drive, and parallel kinematics angle and depth control, with all motors parallel is then shown in Figure 7.4. In this design, the upper motor connects through a bevel gear to a ball screw to convert the rotary motion into vertical motion. For stability is this ball screw is then supported by 2 linear slides. By using linear slides made from IGUS X, it is also possible to maintain a highly precise but low friction slide, that can withstand the sterilisation procedure. This setup is shown in Figure 7.5.

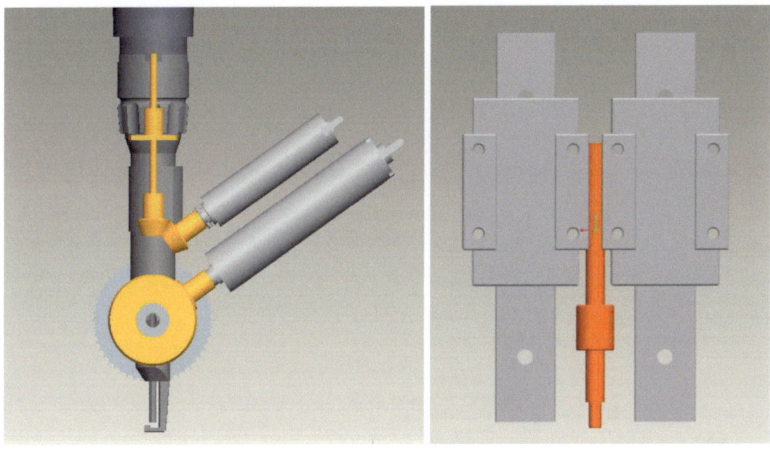

Figure 7.5.: Chosen Motor Layout and Kinematic Construction

7.2. Motor / Gearing Configuration

The exact motor choice was found with standard mechanical calculations from the requirements of the project. Commencing with determination of the power required at the wheel for achieving a 40N cutting force while travelling at 4mm/s a motor with a minimum of 160mW (at the wheel) would be required. See equation 7.1.

$$P_w = Fv \qquad (7.1)$$

The torque at the wheels, with a diameter of 35mm, is then calculated at 700mNm. See equation 7.2.

$$\tau_w = F\frac{D}{2} \qquad (7.2)$$

The required rotational speed of the wheels can also be calculated at 2.18 rpm. See equation 7.3.

$$n_w = \frac{v}{\pi D} \qquad (7.3)$$

To determine the motors required, the following was calculated with inclusion of the bevel gear providing a 3:1 reduction and a 4-stage planetary gear reduction of 275:1. Additionally the following parameters was used:

- Bevel Gear Efficiency $n_B = 0.8$

- Bevel Gear Ratio $i_B = 3$

- Planetary Gear Efficiency $n_P = 0.6$

- Planetary Gear Ratio $i_P = 275$

This implies that the power of the motor must be a minimum of 333.3mW. See Equation 7.4.

$$P_mot = P_w\frac{1}{n_B n_P} \qquad (7.4)$$

The required motor torque, taking into account the gear ratios is therefor 1.77mNm. See Equation 7.5

$$\tau_m ot = \tau_w \frac{1}{n_B n_P i_B i_P} \qquad (7.5)$$

This is required at a motor speed of 1798rpm. See Equation 7.6

$$n_m ot = n_w i_B i_P \qquad (7.6)$$

Because the additional requirements of the system dictate minimum weight for a handheld device, it is advisable here to use the smallest possible motor. For this reason it was decided to proceed with a brushless DC motor with rare earth Neodynium magnets from Maxonmotors©. These motors also have the advantage of a closely integrated planetary gearbox that suited the design choice. The torque curve and operating region of the chosen motor is shown in figure 7.6

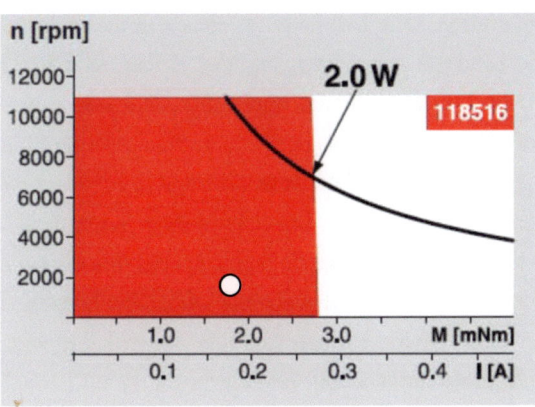

Figure 7.6.: Operating graph for the Maxon Motors RE13, 2 Watt (118516) from Maxon Motor. The required operating point is shown as a white dot.

7.3. Structure Modeling

In the following section, the final CAD model of the developed surgical robot is presented. This involves discussion for development of the overall shape and the design of the individual components. Figure 7.1 has already presented the panoramic view of the robot. The CAD model combined all the principle ideas discussed above, with an overlaid handgrip modeled from transparent plastic to allow visualisation here of the underlying structures. This handgrip could be customised for any individual user or modeled out of a variety of materials to achieve the final desired aesthetics. One possible such option would be a polished wood.

7.3.1. Drive Train implementation

The complete drive train consists of the wheels, bevel gears, the four stage planetary geared motors, the interlinking shafts, and support bearings. Figure 7.7 is a sectional view showing implementation of the wheel bearing setup. The main gear of the bevel gearing and wheel are both supported by this configuration. The two bearings shown at the bottom in green are flanged glide bearings made from Inglidur X from IGUS. This removes any requirement for oil or grease application in a sterile area. The pretensioning of the gearing and wheel is achieved with an axial tightening screw. The exact adjustment of these bearings is achieved with selection and placement of a shim ring during construction. The axle is secured with an interference fit between the axle and housing, this ensures zero movement of the axle during use. Between the wheel and housing an open seal is designed. This is wide enough to allow the moisture and heat during sterilisation to enter without any hindrance, but small enough to prevent any possible metal fragments from the gearing escaping from normal wear during use.

Figure 7.8 shows a sectional view directly through the drive train of the wheels. Seen at the bottom of the illustration are the wheels, their bearings and the bevel gear. The pinion of the bevel gear is mounted at 90° to the wheel axle. Also seen is the motor connectors which are discussed later.

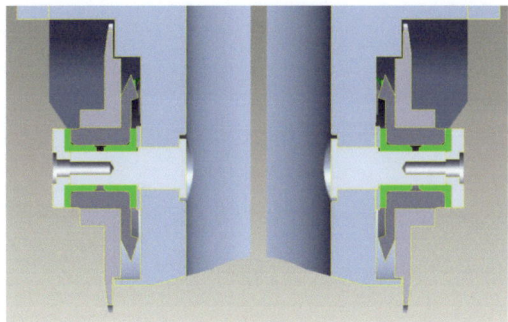

Figure 7.7.: Bearing Setup Surrounding the wheels.

The bearing on the pinion shaft is with a deep groove bearing as fixed bearing together with a glide bearing as floating bearing. The axial fixation of the fixed bearing is achieved with through the grub screw of the bevel gear that pushes axially through a bushing. The fixation of the outside of the fixed bearing is achieved through another bushing that is secured from the cover plate that is screwed down.

7.3.2. Parallel Kinematic Drive Train

In Figure 7.9 the vertical section view through both ball screws is presented. In this figure the ball screw is in the lowest possible position (i.e. the Craniotomy is cutting at its deepest) The maximum stroke of the spindle moves from this position a full 22mm vertically. The screw extends from this position 27mm out of the ball screw nut allowing for a 5mm safety margin. The ball screw nut includes a key that fixates to the housing, thus converting the rotary motion into linear motion. Linear motion between the two sections of the housing is supported with two guide blocks. These guide blocks slide on the guide rails which must be installed parallel to the ball screw axis to avoid any unnecessary lateral forces on the guide elements.

An intermediary shaft connects the ball screw with the bevel gear. The intermediary shaft is connected with the bevel gear and ball screw through

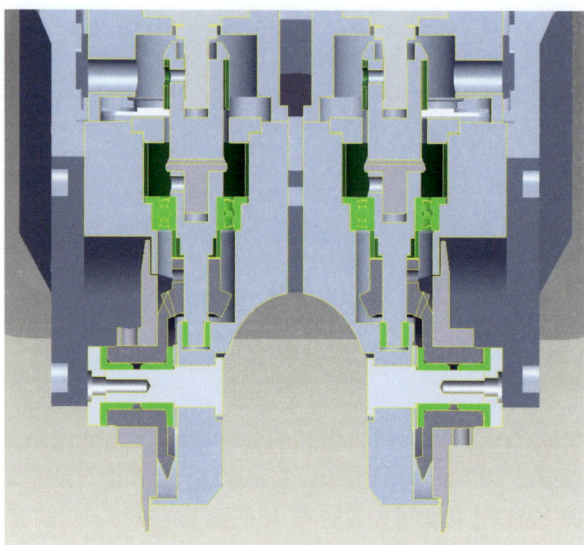

Figure 7.8.: Drive Section Cross Section View.

two grub screws. The ball screw includes a flanged end that better supports the transfer of torques through the screw. This entire axis is again supported by one fixed and one floating bearing. The fixed bearing is a deep groove type that is fixed to the bevel gear through its grub screw.

In Figure 7.13 the lateral sectional view through the drive section of the ball screws is presented. The angle between the two drives is set at 53.13° from the selection of the bevel gearing from Maedler. This angle sets up the angle of both ball screw motors as well as the drive motors, which from the Shaft Connection section, must be parallel. The superposition of the gearing of both bevel gears in each case represents the fixation of the gearing to the larger of the deep groove ball bearings, making it the fixed bearing. Since the drive train of the ball screw can occur at relatively high speeds, the use of plain bearings is avoided. Fixation of the bevel gears with the axle is achieved with grub screws. The bevel gear and the inner ring are separated by shim rings to ensure the setting of the bevel gearing

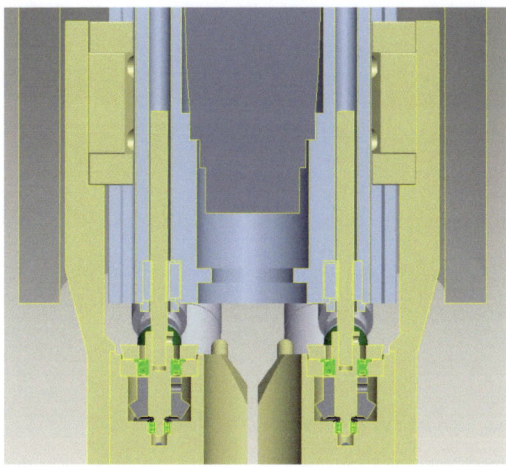

Figure 7.9.: Sectional View through Ball Screw Drive.

has minimum backlash.

A silicon tube is used to seal the lubricated lead screw from the outside. It is clamped on one side between the covers of the ball screw drive nut and the housing. On the other side it is wrapped around the cover of the fixed bearing with a wire and thus pressed on the outside of the lid. For this reason the cover is beveled on its outer side to prevent slippage of the silicon tube.

7.3.3. Motor Housing Connection

Discussed above was the requirement to have a method of disconnecting the motors during sterilisation. Thus the sensitive electronics and encoders could be protected from the heat and moisture. The fundamental solution is shown in Figure 7.11a. The connection required a high probability of connection without user intervention, and a highly stable connection (with zero backlash) achieved with only a press fitting of the parts, i.e. no threading. The connection could also not be clipped together because of the requirement to be able to separate and join the parts a numerous times. This

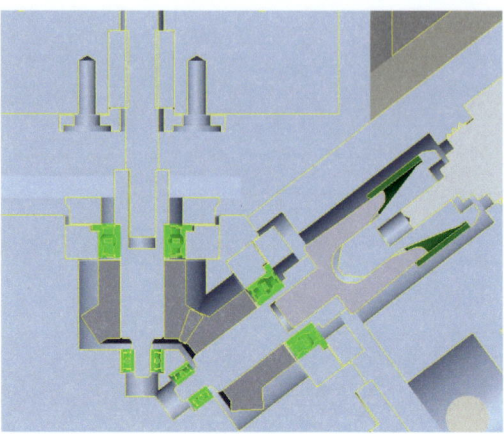

Figure 7.10.: Sectional View through Bearing Setup for Ball Screw Drive.

figure also shows the working surfaces of the assembly, the red surfaces for aligning the two shafts, and the green surfaces, through which the torque is transferred when assembled.

Figure 7.11.: Motor Shaft Connection

Figure 7.11b shows the final assembly, inclusive of the surrounding sleeve. The sleeve ensures the connection remains secure after assembly with external pressure. The fork includes an expansion angle of $1°$ ensuring a countering force.

The end result of all four motors connecting through this system is then shown in 7.12 with the complete motor housing. Discussed here is also the mounting of the motors in this motor housing. The upper of the two motors includes a threaded end for screwed insertion into the motor housing.

The lower motor is fixed with the aid of two screws in the housing. The motors are then fixed to their shaft through a further two screws that are inserted from the side of the housing. The alignment of the motor housing with the main housing is achieved with four guide pins. Because the motor housing is not completely sterile before connection, it is wrapped with a special surgical cloth that is manufactured sterile with correct holes for the alignment pins, connecting shafts, and two screws that fix the two housing parts together once aligned. This cloth then extends up the side of the motor housing, completely wrapping it, and providing a 100% sterile robot for the surgery.

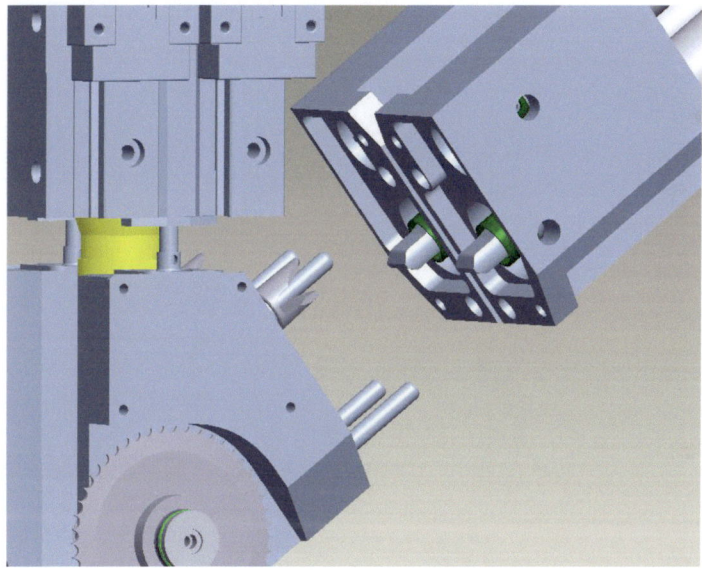

Figure 7.12.: Connection of all Motors in Housing

7.4. Wheel Design

The wheel design was based on the requirements of the skull modeling for what was required to achieve grip. Three designs were first built, one using a simple rough surface (engineered through the process of Knurling), and two built with different sized Spikes. No detailed data for the assessment is provided here, because it was a simple yes / no test result. The knurled wheels were not able to maintain any friction on the skull surface. The two spiked wheels were both able to maintain grip with no difference in performance. Seen in Figure 7.13 is the final design. Here can be seen the 1.5mm spikes, and safety flange that prevents excessive penetration of the wheels on soft skulls. The flange on the inside of the wheel mates with the seal as discussed above in section 7.3.1.

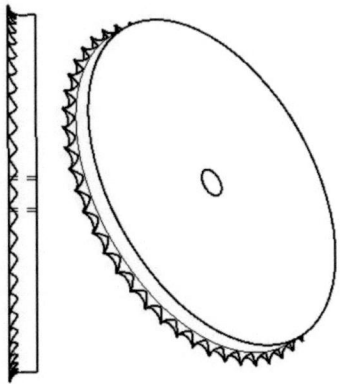

Figure 7.13.: Wheel Design

7.5. Conclusion

The final design has achieved a 100% sterilisable robot, that can be completely built for under 2000€. The four drive axes maintain high efficiency

114

due to the ball bearings and Inglidur X bearings that are able to withstand the high temperatures and humidity of sterilisation.

8. Software Tool

8.1. Background

The following chapter discusses the software implementation of the robot's control system and corresponding graphical user interface (GUI). In maintaining the hardware engineering design concepts of simplicity and integration, the software architecture was designed for implementation of the entire system on a single computer. This is in stark contrast to many other systems mentioned in the State-of-the-Art chapter which discussed the requirement for more complex architectures including optical tracking servers, and separate computers for driving separate GUI / system control loops.

The second important design consideration was in the error handling concepts. It is not intended, that when the system is deployed for use, an engineer is continuously on standby ready to assist the surgeon in solving a problem. For this reason, all errors discovered attempt to solve themselves, with a progressively increasing diagnostics level, and finally a system watchdog is developed external to the computer. This watchdog monitors the entire system for statistical variations in its operation, and is capable of shutting down the robot should inappropriate behaviour be detected. Working together with this error handling and watchdog monitoring, the GUI is kept very simple, only showing critical information for the surgeon. Key to this point, the GUI offers the surgeon a green / red, or go / no-go indicator on overall system readiness.

8.1.1. Loop Speed

Key to this architectural requirement, is that only a low control loop cycle rate (>10Hz) is required for the system. A higher control loop rate is required for the motor speed controllers; however, this is achieved external to the computer. The reason for requiring only a low control loop rate is as follows. Firstly, the overall system is relatively slow with movement speeds less than 4mm/s, and a desired accuracy of 0.5mm, there is only a necessity to have update speeds >8Hz. Secondly, the main source of noise in the system, is that of the human hand holding the device. In previous works this noise is measured to occur at different frequencies, but all are noted as being well below 10Hz. In the work by Harwell and Ferguson[50] they state, quoting from earlier work by Allum et al.[3] that 'A component of physiologic tremor in the frequency range less than 6 Hz arises from drifts in muscle tension when the number of motor units during sustained contractions varies slowly.' Gomez et al.[44] in 1999 and later Riviere and Jensen[100] in 2000 measured this noise and found the noise predominantly below 5Hz for a small surgical instrument. See Figure 8.1

The different parts of the body have different resonant frequencies, the fingers at approximately 25Hz, the wrist at approximately 10Hz, and the forearm at approximately 3Hz. With the use of the Craniostar, the resonant frequency of the fingers is not applicable, and it is only necessary to stay above the resonant rate of the wrist at 10Hz. There is no fixed amount by which this should occur, but for the purpose of safety, a factor of 3 is applied. This safety factor was chosen to allow good syncronisation with the Optical Tracking System operating at 30Hz. The other point to note here, is that due to stabilisation of the robot at two points on the patients skull (i.e. the robot's wheels), all tremor by the surgeons hand, will be directed into the forward / rearward tilt of the robot. This may cause some oscillations in the robot's speed; however, will cause little to no effect on the accuracy of the robot.

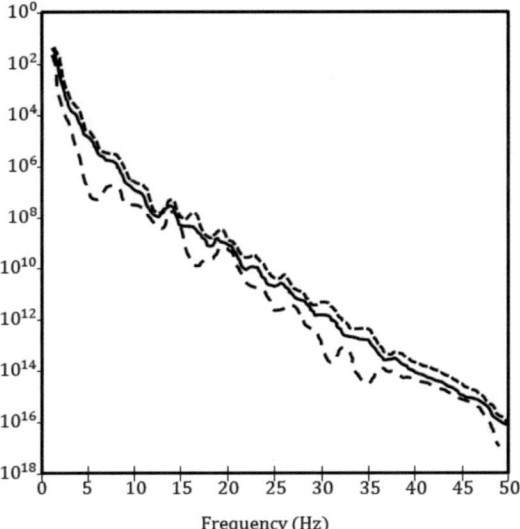

Figure 8.1.: From [100], the noise power from a surgeon's hand tremor holding a light surgical instrument.

8.2. Communications Architecture

As with all Systems Engineering exercises, prior to establishing the software or hardware architecture and requirements, the Interface Control Document (ICD) was developed. This step was also critical in ensuring the integration of the system in the OR components. The key links of this communications requirements are shown in Figure 8.2.

The first step for analysing the communications links left no option in choosing the link protocol. For example, the NDI© Optical Tracking system only has a serial link and the motors from Maxon Motors© use proprietary controllers with CAN or serial links. The option here was taken to use CAN Links for two reasons, firstly the increase in bandwidth of the CAN bus over the serial bus allowed increased control over the motors. For example, this allowed an improved error checking function from the motors. Secondly the CAN bus has an inbuilt error handling protocol, re-

119

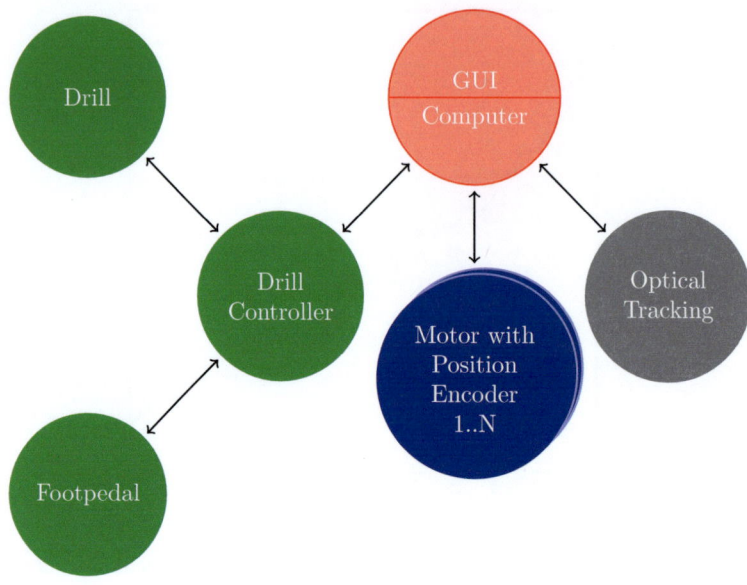

Figure 8.2.: Communications Flow

moving the requirement for forward error correction and message handling routines. The most advantageous point of the CAN bus over a series of serial links, is the shift to a bus protocol, that allows easy extension of the bus without any additional hardware. Any additional serial link, requires additional USB to Serial convertors, and additional handling routines in the computer. Because the project was always viewed as advancing from a 2 DOF robot to a 4 DOF robot, this choice was clear.

More complicated was the interface to the Drill Controller. The Aesculap Microdrive used does not include any embedded interface capability. As such, an interface box was required to enable control over the drill speed, and for feedback for the drill torques.

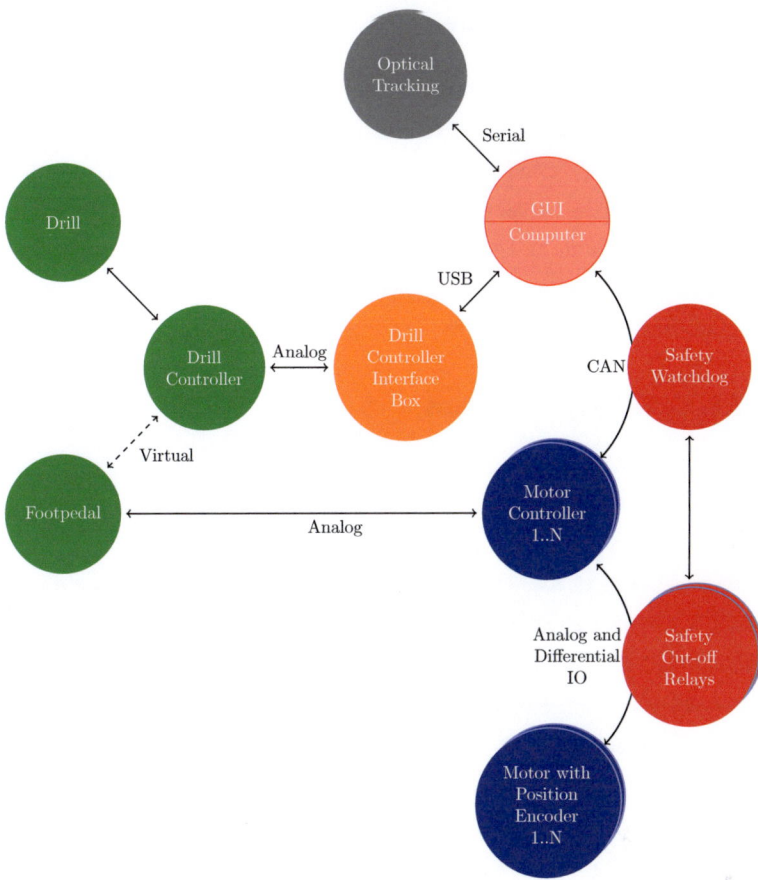

Figure 8.3.: Communications Architecture of final design. The inclusion of the red items, the Safety Watchdog and Safety Cutout Relays are discussed in Chapter 10.2.4.

8.3. Software Architecture

As with all system architectures, there is a series of startup routines and main process routines. The startup routines are concerned with the loading of trajectory data, marker data, visualisation meshes for the GUI, as well as the startup routines for all the communications links. These are considered standard procedure, and no further time is spent discussing their implementation here. Instead, this chapter will concentrate on the core system control thread, as well as the implementation of the GUI.

8.3.1. Core System Threads

The core of the system runs on three thread loops. Two threads are concerned with the control loop, the third is for the GUI and event handling.

The two threads for the control loop are split primarily because of the slow processing of the serial communications to the Optical Tracking. As such, a single loop is used to continually poll the optical tracking loop for updated position information. When new data is received, this data is passed off to the second control thread, for processing; while the first loop immediately requests new data from the serial communications.

The second control thread is then concerned with using the updated position information, to implement the control algorithms in accordance with Chapter 6. This thread is also involved with the error handling from the control loop and the downstream CAN links. The concept of the interlocking loops is shown in Figure 8.4.

8.3.2. Error Handling

In order to keep the system intuitive for the surgeon, it is essential that all possible error handling occurs automatically by the system. An example for this is shown in Figure 8.6.

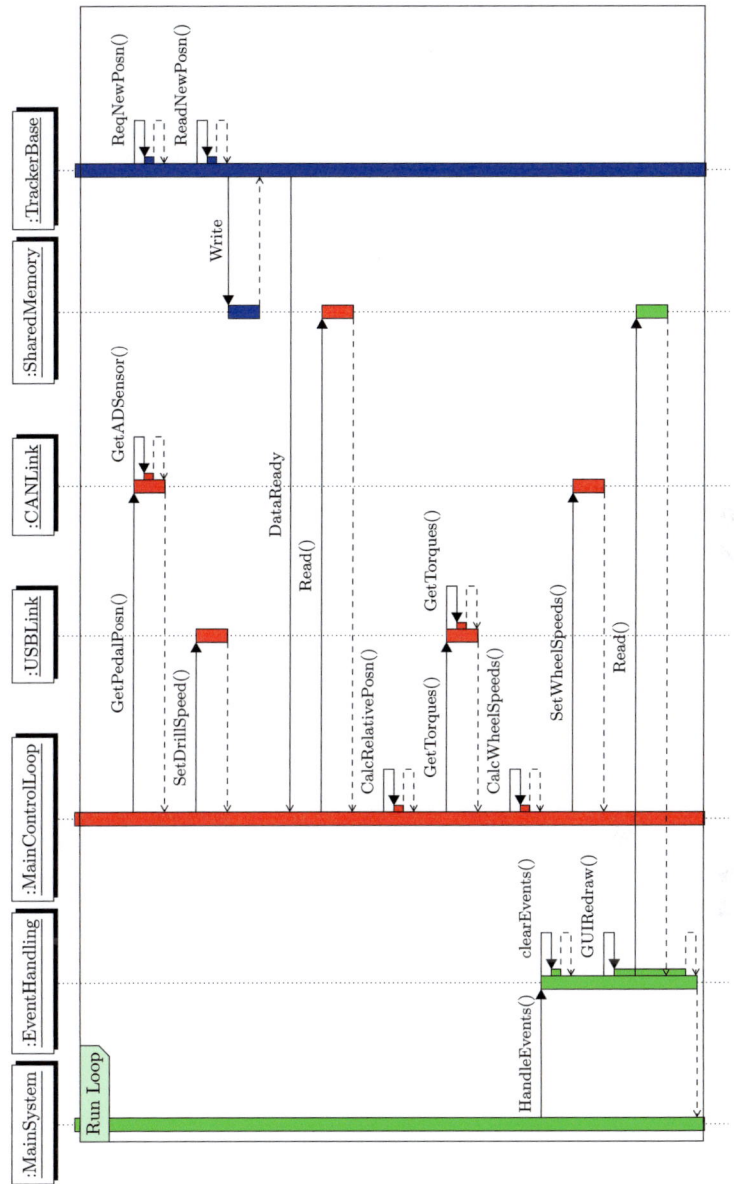

Figure 8.4.: Thread Syncronisation

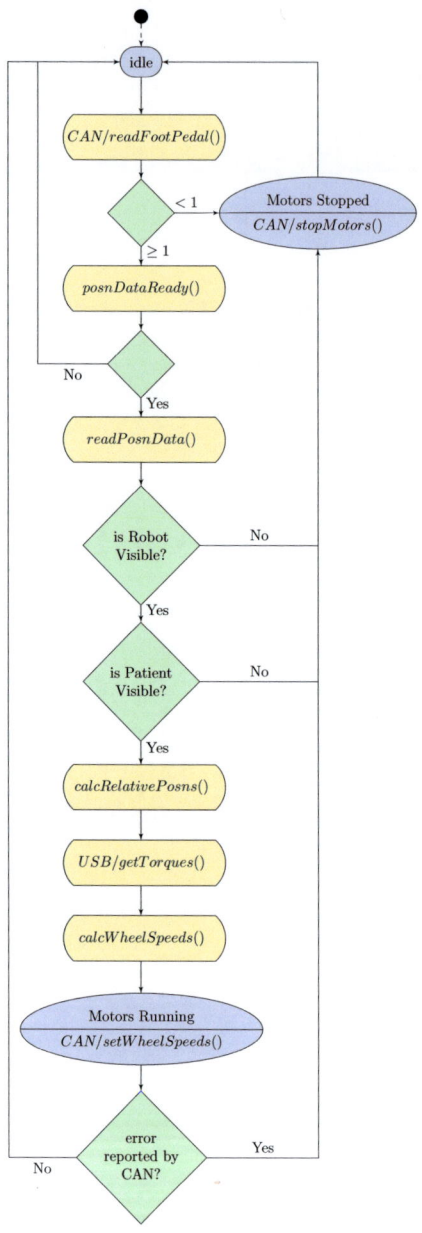

Figure 8.5.: Main Control Loop Process

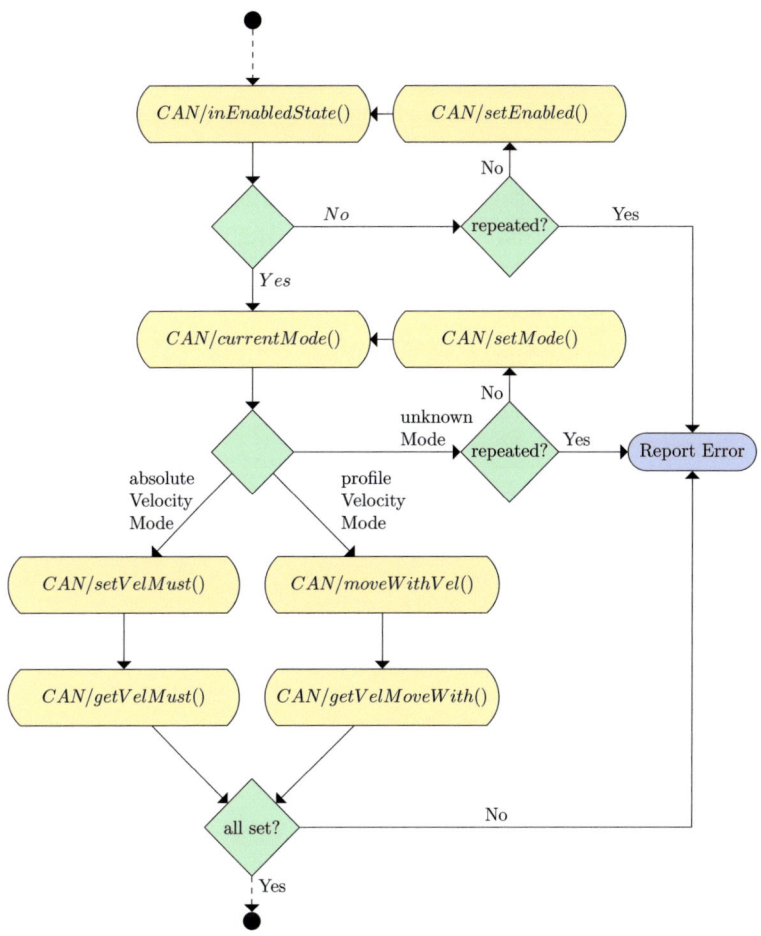

Figure 8.6.: Error Checking in Set Velocity command for motors. (Occurs for left and right motors)

8.3.3. Graphical User Interface

The GUI was designed from the start to end to be solely a visual feedback system. There is a highly limited ability to input any commands while the program is running. It is strictly limited to the ability to move between a calibration mode / registration mode to the run-time robot control mode. The following chapter on Surgeon Interaction outlines the design of this GUI.

9. Interaction with the Surgeon

The interaction with the surgeon is a clearly important section for this project, but due to the push for intuitive control, it is also maintained as a highly simplistic solution. The following chapter outlines the two sections of surgeon interaction; firstly the GUI with which the surgeon can see the operating state of the robot, and secondly the velocity control of the robot.

9.1. GUI

As already mentioned, the GUI is presented in a highly simplistic manner. For the main section of the operation, it contains only two visual sections, only one interactive component and is built completely using the Visualisation Toolkit (VTK) (www.vtk.org). Figure 9.1 shows this GUI. The main component is the visual indicator for how the craniotomy cut is proceeding along the planned trajectory. The secondary visual section below, provides an overview of the system components. The one interactive component is for moving between the calibration / registration mode, and the normal Craniotomy mode. This allows the surgeon to redo any phase of the calibration / registration if either of these elements is later deemed unacceptable. This mode change is achieved with the cursor keys on the normal keyboard, and thus must be performed by an assisting nurse to ensure the surgeon remains sterile. Of note here, it would be possible to build any sterile controller for such a system at a later date if this was desired.

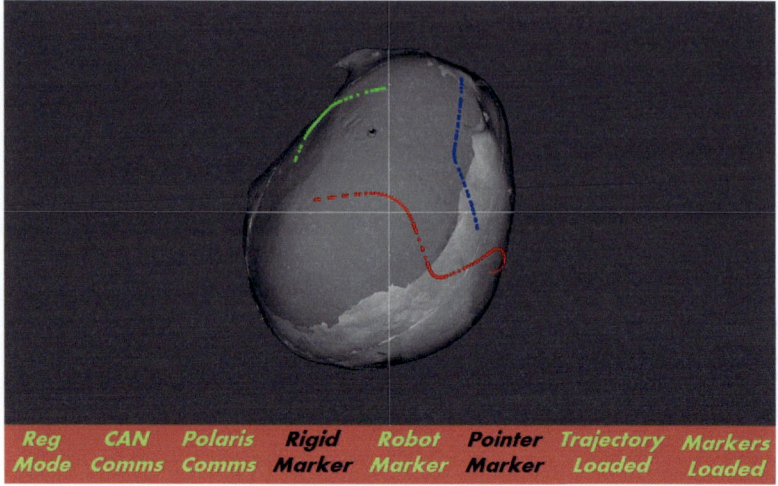

Figure 9.1.: GUI for system use

9.1.1. Main Visual Component - During Craniotomy

This visual component provides a feedback of the robot position on the trajectory. It is achieved through the vtkCamera class, with the position defined as the top of the cutting axis, the look at point is the tip of the cutting axis, and the up direction, is the forward direction of the robot. A cross hairs overlay provides a clear indication of the centre of this picture, and the trajectory is shown as a series of points, 1mm in diameter. This allows for a clear indication of how accurately the robot is actually cutting.

9.1.2. Main Visual Component - During Calibration and Registration

The main visual component for calibration and registration provides a series of static pictures of the target or item that needs to be pivoted. These pictures are produced prior to the operation. They can also include static text providing help on what needs to be calibrated or registered. Figure 9.3

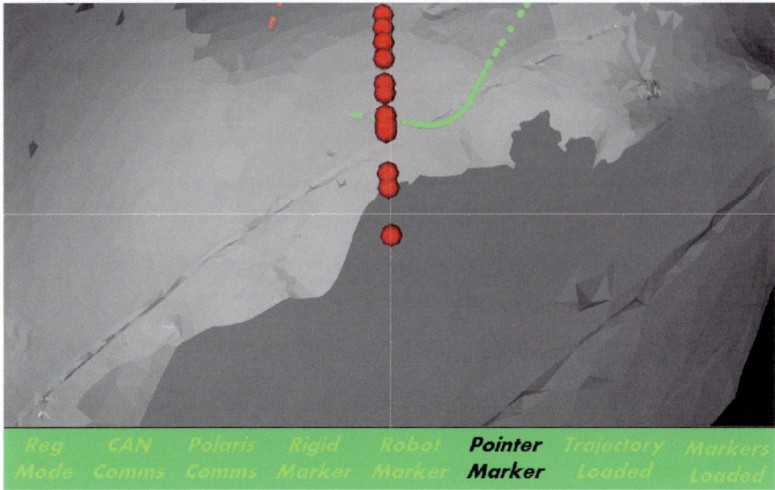

Figure 9.2.: GUI system, with robot held near start point of trajectory

provides two example pictures, one from a calibration and one from a registration. The feedback to the registration and calibration comes as per during the procedure from the secondary screen component.

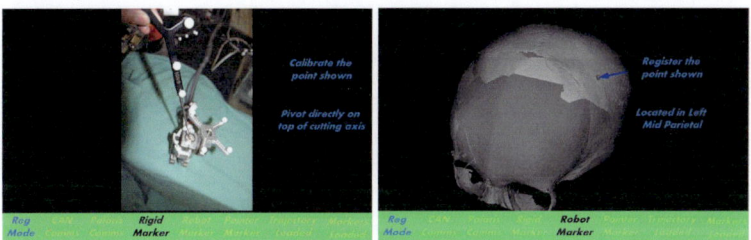

Figure 9.3.: Calibration / Registration GUI images

9.1.3. Secondary Visual Component

The second section provides the update on the system status to the Surgeon throughout all phases of the system usage. This component entails simply the lower section of the screen as seen in 9.4. Each system component is represented by its name, and the color indicates whether it is working or not. The background for this section then provides a complete 'one look' system status, Green indicates that everything is okay, Red indicates that a problem exists and the surgeon should not proceed to use the system. Because all possible error checking and error recovery already exists in the software, the only additional repair / recovery options available to the surgeon are to check that all the cables are correctly plugged in, and that the Optical Tracking System is turned on. For this reason, there is no requirement to include any interactable configuration in this section of the GUI. This is also due to the system being closed to the surgeon. For example, the communications ports to be used are all fixed in the configuration files, baud rates etc are all optimised and are not to be changed by the surgeon during an operation.

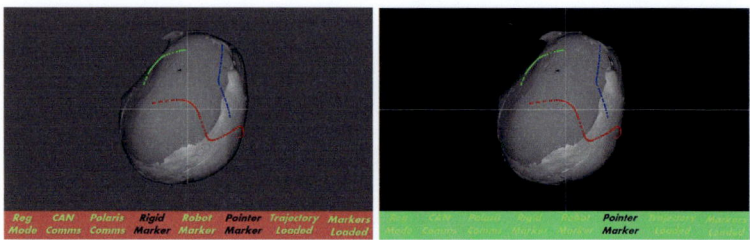

Figure 9.4.: Functioning / In Error Demonstration of System Secondary Visual Component

9.2. Velocity Control Calibration

As discussed in the chapter on the steering control system, and specifically seen in Figure 6.5, the surgeon sets the desired speed of the robot predominantly through the lean of the drill. The intuitive action of pushing and pulling the robot sets this lean as the robot tilts over its wheel axle. Figure

6.5 had shown however, that the actual desired velocity command v^* is determined with the use of three Gain terms, G_a, G_b and G_c. This sets up how sensitive the robot is to the leaning as well as the sensitivity to the torque of the drill. In practice it was determined that different surgeons liked using the robot with different sensitivities. It was therefore setup as a configurations parameter loaded at the start of the procedure for the operating physician.

9.3. Workflow and Calibration

Appendix 1 to this thesis includes a workflow description of the standard craniotomy procedure for a child with Craniosynostosis. The only two modifications required for implementation with this robot are shown in Table 9.1.

9.3.1. Modification for steps prior to surgery

Previously, the surgeon had many options for planning the surgery, for example:

1. Drawing on X-Ray images.

2. Making physical measurements from patient.

3. Using a Computer Aided Surgery Planning Computer with the aid of CT imagery.

4. Using experience.

In order to employ this approach, it is however necessary to restrict the planning to a specific software set that is capable of outputting the correctly formatted data for the registration and trajectories. In this system I have employed the KASOP System that was previously developed within our institute. This software takes the segmented CT data, and allows the

Table 9.1.: Modifications for Workflow

Modified Workflow Step	Old Step Actions	New Step Actions
Prior to Surgery 1	Pre-operative imaging is taken for patient	Surgeon conducts local operation to insert titanium markers for registration, then pre-operative imaging is taken for patient.
Prior to Surgery 2	Surgeon plans surgery on X-Ray images, or on computer with CT imagery	Surgeon plans surgery on computer with CT imagery. Trajectory data is then saved, inclusive of patient registration data extracted from CT.
Prior to Surgery 3	High Speed Drill is sterilised.	Robot is sterilised, robot motor housing is wrapped in sterile cloth and attached to main robot section. Robot is calibrated.
6	Surgeon draws plan onto skull.	Surgeon performs registration of patient.
7	Bore holes are drilled through the skull along drawn plan.	Bore holes are drilled through the skull along trajectory using GUI and optically tracked pointer for guidance.
10	Craniotomy is performed, linking bore holes.	Craniotomy is performed using Robot.

surgeon to prepare the surgical plan using either a normal computer mouse, a 6D mouse or a variety of haptic interface devices. While there is no automatic segmentation of the titanium markers from within KASOP, it does allow the surgeon to identify the pivot points manually. The final steps before the surgery is the assembly of the robot, and its calibration. The assembly is discussed in section 7.3.3. The only step then remaining is the calibration. Because of the ease at which this calibration can occur, it can be completed before the surgery, or even when the surgeon first takes hold of the device prior to use, as part of the registration. It is however outlined for completion here, as part of the system startup to ensure that everything is working prior to the surgery.

Calibration of Device

The process involves two pivotisations, and one known movement. The first step involves removal of the end piece of the craniotomy tool, such that a pivotisation can be performed directly on the end of the drill piece. From the definitions of Section 6.2 this defines the drill tip, defined $\mathscr{C}_{\mathscr{T}}$, to the computer.

The second pivotisation is performed by the optically tracked pointer directly on the top of the craniotomy tool without the cable connection. This defines the point $\mathscr{C}_{\mathscr{Y}}$, which is the top of the drill. These two points together have already defined the cutting axis of the robot $\overrightarrow{\mathscr{C}_{\mathscr{A}}}$.

The final stage involves the definition of the forward vector of the robot. In this stage the robot is held on the base of the box in which it was sterilised, and the robot moves forwards approximately 5cm. This motion is tracked by the computer and the forward vector recorded.

9.3.2. Step 6 Modifications

In this step, the surgeon commences with the registration of the patient as per a normal IGS operation. Markers screws are pivoted in the order indicated through the system GUI. Following this the optically tracked pointer is traced around the inside of the skin flap of the patient. This line is later used for the safety margin for the robot and is discussed more later in section 10.1.

9.3.3. Step 7 Modifications

In this step, the surgeon holds the robot over where he thinks the trajectory will go, confirms this location with the GUI that is aligned with the robot, refines the position of the robot, and then underneath where the robot was held, the surgeon drills each hole. It is acknowledged that this step is comparatively slower than before; however, it is necessary to ensure free movement of the robot along the trajectory that it will not be hindered by Dura Mater still affixed to the underside of the skull.

9.3.4. Step 10 Modifications

This step is the main use of the Craniotomy Robot, and as the target of this entire thesis, is not discussed here.

9.4. Conclusion

This chapter has outlined how the system interacts with the surgeon. The simplistic GUI ensures the surgeon can concentrate on the surgery and not on the system configuration or other details. The GUI also provides a very clear indication to the surgeon on the overall state of the system. A Green or Red background to the status information tells the surgeon if the system is functioning correctly and whether the system is able to be used or not.

The final section of the chapter outlined the required workflow modifications required by the surgeon for implementing the system. With the exception of the calibration and registration, the main changes are in the pre-operative stage for the planning.

10. Safety System and Risk Analysis

As with all medical projects a thorough risk analysis was completed, concentrating on not only technical issues and failures, but additionally procedural and workflow issues. The risk analysis completed was a three layer deep failure analysis. In this analysis, all possible failures were identified, and all possible combinations of the failures were identified that could occur simultaneously. For example, the tracking system reports false positions, the speed pedal locks-on, and the safety stop button fails to work all simultaneously. The likelihood of occurrence was then combined with the possible outcome through a standard risk analysis nomogram, to determine the level of risk, from low through to catastrophic. While the complete risk analysis is not included here, there were two regions of failure that due to such a resulting high risk level, required modification. One of these was procedural, and one of these was technical. This chapter outlines the problems that led to the requirements for modification, and the applied solutions.

10.1. Procedural Modification - Confirmation of Safety Zone

One procedural problem, alone or in cooperation with other problems that was seen to contribute to a high risk level was simply the failure of an accurate registration. This problem alone was seen to lead to a number of small problems such as the undesired prolonging of the operation, due to the requirement to recomplete sections of the craniotomy or in the worst case the complete craniotomy again. When the desired surgery is the removal of tumorous bone identified in a CT scan, the failure to remove the correct bone could also lead to the requirement for a completely new surgery later, combined with more CTs and more radiation. Additional problems occurring as a result could involve the robot attempting to drive over the drawn back skin flaps, damaging the soft-tissue and periosteum that could affect the ability of the patient to recover after the surgery.

10.1.1. Discussion of the Problem

The problem lies with the possible poor registration of the rigid body on the patient. As discussed in section 2.2.2 and 2.2.6, the registration is completed using the 'Gold Standard' method for IGS. Whereby an optical tracking marker is 'Pivoted' on the top of 3 or more Titanium screws that were inserted prior to imaging, and whose positions were determined in segmentation during planning.

The problem here is not necessarily the accuracy of the procedure, there are many papers (e.g. [7] and [32]) that report this procedure can achieve registration down to < 2mm in the area local to the titanium screws. The problem is more the possibility that the procedure simply has not worked. For example, if the screws are registered in the false order, the registration can be rotated by 90 or 180 degrees. Depending on the layout pattern of the screws this can also result in a more subtle registration error that is not easily identifiable. Because this problem can occur as part of a procedural error, the increasing of the number of screws used for registration will also not necessarily improve the result, though as per the previous papers on registration techniques this is always recommended.

Additionally, any possible technique for confirming the registration, through pointing at additional markers does not fix the procedural problem. Though for certain instances it can reduce the likelihood. The alternate possibilities for confirming the registration was seen in combining the point registration with a surface registration. Discussed later, this also provided a significant advantage in defining a safety region for the robot.

10.1.2. Discussion of combination with a Surface Matching Registration

Surface matching registration is an accepted alternate concept to point-point registration within the field of Maxillo-Facial and Cranial Surgeries, with different advantages and disadvantages. Discussed in many papers such as [103], surface registration using a laser pointer such as the Z-Touch©from Brainlab is seen as less accurate than pair-point registration, but gains advantages by being non-contact, this leads to less chance of infection etc. More advanced methods such as surface matching with laser scanning can offer nearly the same accuracy as the point-point registration[98], but the equipment is significantly more expensive. This surface scanning is also more typically used for the facial region, where the contours in areas such as nose and orbital rim / forehead are significantly more pronounced. It is less common for the cranial region.

Surface matching techniques are also reliant here on the Iterative Closest Point (ICP) algorithm for determining the match between the two surfaces. Because this is an iterative technique, it is highly reliant on the first guess of the alignment of the two surfaces.

For generation of a combined registration technique here, in the workflow analysis is was noted that the registration occurs after the pulling back of the skin fold for exposing the skull. This provides one advantage that the surface matching occurs on the bone surface, and not on the soft tissue exterior. This removes any soft tissue registration problems, where the soft tissue has moved since imaging, due to additional swelling of the patient, or simply a different laying position of the patient. However, a new problem is that the skull region is surrounded by the skin fold. This skin fold is significantly large in comparison to the area of exposed skull. This skin fold would therefore require an initial segmentation algorithm, followed by application of the ICP. [78][70] Additionally, the combining of multiple registration systems and hardware would increase the number of

137

inter-hardware registration errors. While the individual registration errors may still be small from each individual hardware component, this has the possibility of increasing the overall system error. This can occur when each registration value must be transformed into the optical tracking coordinate system (world coordinates) as required by the system controller, and each of the transformation matrixes created through equipment calibration have additional errors.

10.1.3. Solution to contour definition and a Surface Matching Registration

The solution provided here combines the point-point registration technique with an intuitive surface matching registration in a single step. After conducting the point-point registration, the surgeon is to use the same pointer to trace out the bone surface along the inside contour of the skin fold. See Figure 10.1. This surface is then used to match against the surface of the skull in a CT. This concept provides a few significant advantages.

Firstly, the surface matching coordinate system is exactly the same as that used for the point-point registration. Therefore, the start position for the ICP algorithm is already given. This is the key note, that this is used to confirm registration, and not generate registration. When the ICP algorithm attempts to move the transformation between the given surfaces more than a threshold value, then the surgeon is warned that a problem has occurred. The surgeon is given a choice to accept the registration of the point-point registration, the surface scan registration, or a chance to repeat either or both of the registration procedures.

Secondly, both registrations occur with the completely same pieces of equipment, even the same pointer. Therefore there are no additional sources of error from additional translation matrixes.

Additionally, the contouring of the skin fold provides two more safety features for the robot control. Firstly it is possible to determine if the skin

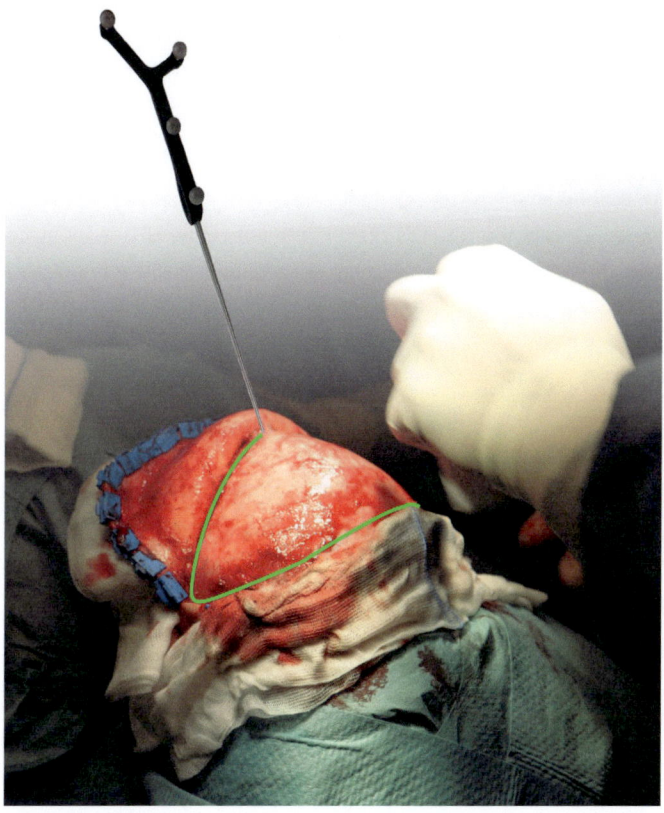

Figure 10.1.: Path (in green) to be lightly traced by Surgeon with Optically Tracked Pointer used in Surface Matching Registration Confirmation and defining the absolute safety region for Robot.

fold is far enough from the planned craniotomy trajectory that the robot can complete the cutting without hindrance. This is a step to again preventing unwanted prolonging of the operation by having to extend the skin flap separation in the middle of the operation when it is realised that the robot will not proceed further without driving over the skin flap. This is shown visually after the surgeon accepts the registration. Secondly by using this contour as a final safety boundary, it is possible to provide a further realtime check that the robot is proceeding correctly. If it is identified that the robot will move outside this scanned contour, the robot is automatically stopped, the surgeon warned about what is happening, and given the option to override this check, or move the robot back into the safety region.

10.1.4. Summary of Procedural Modification

The procedural modification involves the tracing of the skin fold with the optically tracked pointer. This is used for three things:

1. It defines a region within which the robot may move safely.

2. It confirms the point-point registration.

3. It confirms that enough of the surface of the skull has been exposed that the robot may complete the craniotomy trajectory without hindrance from the skin flap.

This technique has the following advantages:

1. The procedure is very fast.

2. The procedure is very intuitive for the surgeon to complete.

3. The ICP algorithm used is very stable given that the initial guess is provided by the first point-point algorithm.

4. There are no additional translations or calibrations to be completed as only the single optically tracked pointer is used.

The one disadvantage noted is that it does now involve move contact with the outside surface of the skull. However, in consultation with the surgeons, due to the fact that the same pointer is already used for the point-point registration, this disadvantage is quite minimum when viewed in context of the entire procedure being undertaken by the patient.

10.2. Technical Modification - Confirmation of Correctly Functioning System

For the benefit of ease of system development, the control system was developed on a Microsoft Windows©PC. This one design choice does however lead to two significant constraints in terms of system reliability. The main constraint is that reliability cannot be guaranteed, and the secondly the system is not real-time. After a complete Risk analysis was completed, there was one problem / failure path identified that could lead to a catastrophic failure. This following section outlines the problem situation, and the safety watchdog system that was built to remedy the problem.

10.2.1. Discussion of the Problem

The problem occurs due to the separated run-time looping of the main control software and the PID velocity control loop in the motor controllers.

When the control software on the Windows©PC crashes there are a number system safety functions that no longer function:

1. The target wheel velocity is no longer calculated and no longer sent to the PID controllers.

2. The speed control due to tilting of the robot does not work.

3. The on-off activation of the robot control does not function because the input from the foot pedal is not detected.

4. The safety area checking described in the above section is not calculated.

The biggest implication of this, is that the PID controllers continue to
operate at the last velocity they have received before the software crash.
This could be straight ahead at full speed, or after a short correction it
could be turning outwards towards the skin fold. This will only be stopped
when the surgeon realises there is a problem and pushes the emergency
stop button. When testing the robot, it was noticed that due to the system's
infancy and the surgeon's lack of knowledge of the system, they were not
sure if the robot was functioning normally, or just slowly, and hence were
hesitant to hit the emergency stop button. Because the robot is capable of
moving at 5mm/s, this led to the robot travelling significantly outside the
safety region before it was stopped. It was therefore decided to implement
a Safety Watchdog system that could monitor the system and should poor
or failing performance be detected, stop the robot.

10.2.2. Discussion of Safety Watchdog Requirements

From the above section, we have now declared two separate safety regions.
One is the ±0.5mm channel along the planned trajectory, and the second
is the safety region before damage occurs to the skin flap and periosteum.
While it is seen as ideal to stop the robot before it goes outside the planned
trajectory channel, it is not actually possible. The robot controller was
tuned to stay within this channel, but it was able to approach the limit of
±0.5mm. This means that any system requirement to stay within this channel would have to stop the robot instantly if something could go wrong.
This leads to further requirements of infinite deceleration which is also not
possible.

The same concept can be carried through to the other safety boundary
at the skin flap. It is checked if the trajectory can be completed with the
robot staying inside the skin flap, but it is possible to approach this bound-

ary limit. In order to define a physical limit within which a system must work, it therefore becomes necessary to define a third safety limit. This was determined in consultation with the surgeons to be a maximum of 2mm outside of the ±0.5mm planned trajectory channel. In accordance with the Fitzpatrick equation, 2mm is the likely accuracy of the registration over the entire head. As the accepted standard accuracy figure, the Surgeons take this into account by normal IGS planning, therefore if the robot stays within this margin, any possible damage from complete failure would be minimal.

Using this 2mm safety margin, and with a maximum robot speed of 5mm/s, it therefore becomes necessary to be able to identify a failure and respond to it within 400ms.

From the initial conception it was decided that any additional safety components would need to be external to the Windows PC. This was because the initial problem is software centric, and it was required that the watchdog system should not be affected by the same crash. The two main requirements for the Safety Watchdog were reliability and simplicity.

One point noted here was that data checking would also be unadvisable. It is of course possible to design a data checking system that would check for malformed data that would possibly lead to downstream problems; however, to implement a thorough enough checker was seen as going against the simplicity requirement. Another concept investigated was the possibility of monitoring a "I am working okay" signal transmitted from the computer. Unfortunately this was also seen as unacceptable because there were identified a number of possibilities where this signal could be transmitted, even when the velocity command outputs were not being calculated correctly or output.

It was seen best to directly monitor the velocity command outputs being sent to the PID controllers. However, without actually performing any data checking on the outputs, they could only be checked on whether they were sent or not. This did however open up an opportunity to monitor the health of the program statistically. Both of these reasons then led to the idea to implement an FPGA controller. An FPGA implemented directly in hardware (i.e. no embedded processor) was seen as beneficial for a number of reasons:

1. The system operates in real-time, with ns resolution.

2. The system is able to control physical outputs (e.g. relays or breaking resistors) with μs response times.

3. The architecture is provable in terms of response times.

4. The system is highly stable.

5. Boot time is measured in ms.

10.2.3. Statistical Monitoring of System

To determine the standard behaviour of the system, a logging system was established to record the timings of transmissions on the CAN bus. [1] The expected response was to see two significant timing gaps, a series of short gaps between answer and response communications, and then a larger gap between frames. In more detail these were estimated as follows:

1. Get Pedal Position Request

2. Pedal Position Answer < 2ms

3. Get Motor Torque, Motor 1 < 10ms

4. Motor Torques Answer, Motor 1 < 2ms

5. Get Motor Torque, Motor 2 < 2ms

---

[1]Note: The CAN is a bidirectional bus, therefore without decoding the bus, it is not possible to determine whether a bus communications is transmitted from the computer to motor controller or vice versa. Therefore, transmission in this discussion involves both transmission and reception of CAN communications by the computer.

6. Motor Torques Answer, Motor 2 < 2ms

7. Get Motor Mode, Motor 1 < 2ms

8. Motor Mode Answer, Motor 1 < 2ms

9. Get Motor Mode, Motor 2 < 2ms

10. Motor Mode Answer, Motor 2 < 2ms

11. Set Motor Velocity, Motor 1 < 2ms

12. Motor Velocity Command Confirmed, Motor 1 < 2ms

13. Set Motor Velocity, Motor 2 < 2ms

14. Motor Velocity Command Confirmed, Motor 2 < 2ms

15. Frame delay to next Get Pedal Position Request > 20ms

This was nearly correct, with the exception that occasionally a longer delay due to the non-real time nature of Windows. The delays, approximately once every second could be up to 200ms long. This is shown in Figure 10.2 and in histogram form in Figure 10.3. In all the measurements it was found that no delay during standard operation occurred longer than 250ms. If a timeout occurred longer than 250ms, a trigger could be used to signal a stop, and this would still provide 150ms for deceleration and stopping.

10.2.4. Solution to System Monitoring

The solution to the above discussion was implemented on a single standalone PCB, with a single Spartan 3A FPGA from Xilinx©. The FPGA listened to the CAN communications through the circuit shown in Figure 10.4. This circuit isolates the FPGA from the CAN communications, and along with standard EMC/EMI design prevents spurious transmissions onto the bus that could lead to more problems. The actual timeout controller

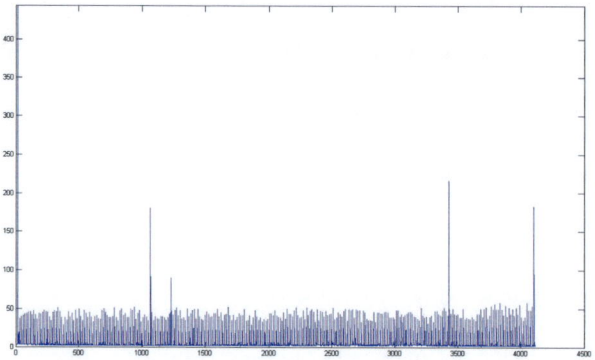

Figure 10.2.: Delays between consecutive CAN Transmissions

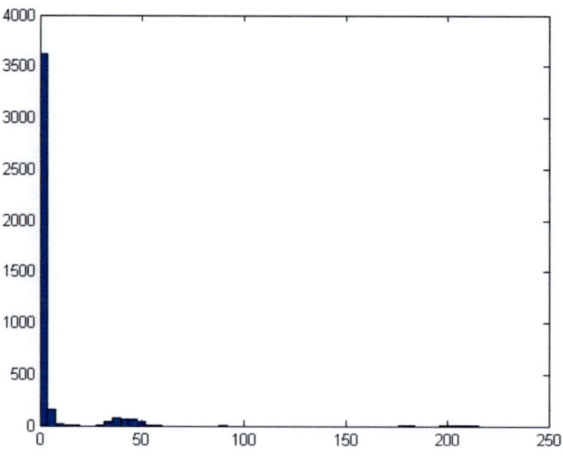

Figure 10.3.: Histogram showing three significant delays between CAN Transmissions, main block < 5ms, secondary block ≈ 30ms, final block ≈ 200ms

schematic and associated VHDL code is then shown in Figure 10.6. The output from the timeout is shown used in Figure 10.5 to directly trigger three relays that were placed inline between the PID motor controllers and the motors. On the alternate side of the relay were braking resistors cabled in to assist in the deceleration. [2]

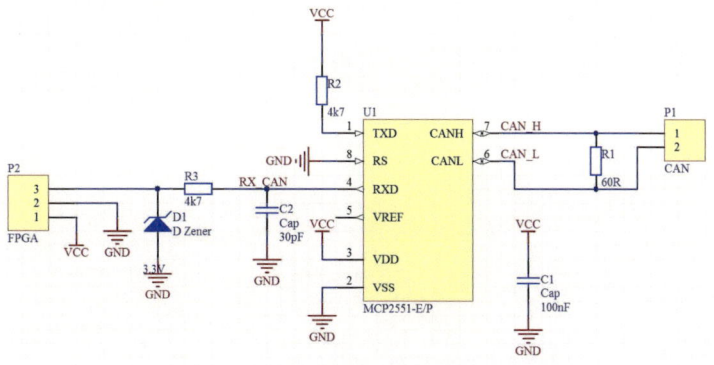

Figure 10.4.: Read only CAN Listener Circuit

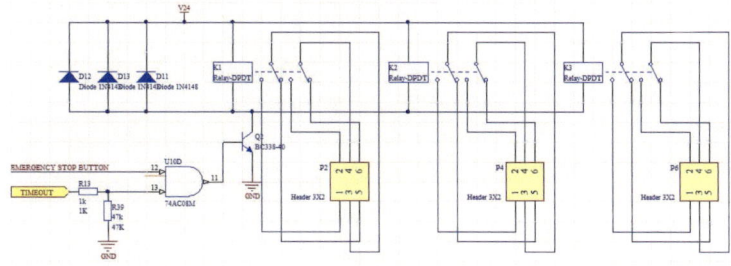

Figure 10.5.: Relay Control from Timeout and Emergency Stop Button. Relays were inline with three phase motor cabling.

---

[2]These were found to make no measurable difference to the rate of deceleration, deemed unnecessary and later removed.

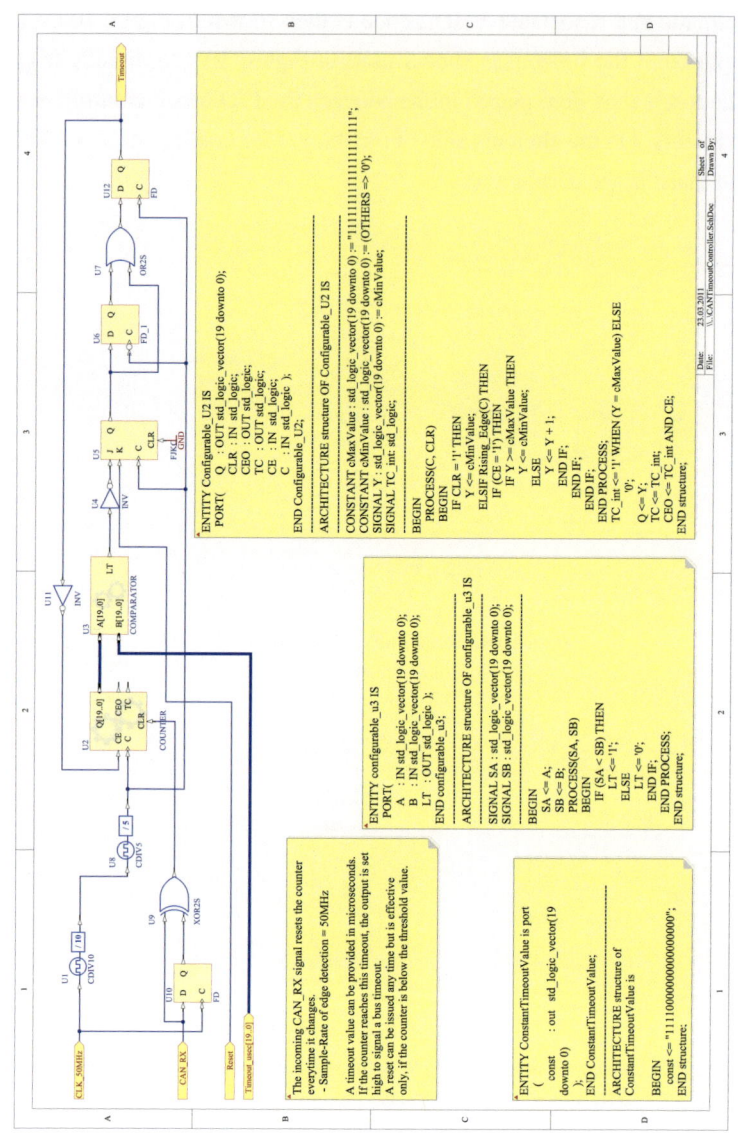

Figure 10.6.: Schematic and VHDL Code for CAN Timeout Safety Watchdog

10.2.5. Summary of Technical Modification

The technical modification involved the successful implementation of a system monitor that monitors the final communications stage of the complete system. Implemented on a single PCB with an FPGA, it was found to be highly stable and proved to successfully stop the system within milliseconds of a software crash. Unfortunately there was no method for determining the actual ability of the system to stop within the given 2ms as this also meant that the tracking system was lost.

Future enhancements for Safety Watchdog

The implemented system in the FPGA was simple, but provided a great deal of flexibility such that additional checks could be included in parallel in the future. The final solution implemented on the FPGA used $< 1\%$ of the available resources. Additional solutions increasing the monitoring could all be implemented in parallel, without affecting the reliability of each watchdog system. One specific idea for consideration is in monitoring the CAN data, and when no data comes for more than 50ms (i.e. a possible long pause from the computer is expected) the watchdog could inject new velocity commands to the motors to slow the wheels down, proportionally for each wheel maintaining the current curve radius, thus decreasing any damage should the system have crashed.

11. Experiences and Evaluation

The following chapter provides the conclusion to trials with the robot prototype. Included here are the accuracy assessment, and impact assessment together with a user evaluation.

11.1. Accuracy assessment

11.1.1. Accuracy assessment methodology

The accuracy of the cutting was completed with two methodologies (online and offline), and in three stages of increasing surface and trajectory complexity. The offline testing involved a post-cut analysis of the cuts, to determine the complete system accuracy. The online testing involved logging the reported accuracy of the tracking system to determine the ability of the control loop to remove any error reported in the tracking system. The complete testing procedure for the offline assessment, with the workflow, shown is follows: (Note: Steps 1-6 simulate a normal pre-operative procedure, with the exception that the laser scan replaces the CT for pre-operative imaging., Step 7 is then the normal use of the system. Only steps 8-14 are the custom measurement procedures used here.)

1. Laser scan surface for cutting.

2. Convert scan into vtkPolyData.

3. Load data into Surgery Planning Software, KASOP.

4. Extract markers for point to point registration of target.

5. Plan trajectory to be performed.

6. Export Surface Data, Markers and Trajectory Data for control system.

7. System is used for performing trajectory cut.

8. Laser scan surface again for assessment.

9. Reduce and Filter Scan data from over 1,000,000 points to approximately 20,000 triangles using GeoMagic Wrap.

10. Convert scan into vtkPolyData.

11. Load both data scanned sets into Vistrails.

12. Load trajectory into Vistrails, superimposed with two Glyphs, 1mm, and 2mm.

13. Trajectory plan is registered with post cut laser scan, through surface to surface registration of first and second laser scans.

14. Manual evaluation is performed for whether or not the trajectory was performed inside or outside the 1mm or 2mm Glyphs.

The end phase of this assessment is shown in Figure 11.1.

11.1.2. Equipment Used

Laser Scanner

The Laser Scanner used is the Laser Line Probe from Faro©, capable of capturing 19200 points / second, made up from 640 points / line at 30 lines per second. The Laser Line Probe has an accuracy of $\pm35\mu$m. This is mounted on the Platinum Faro Arm, with an accuracy of 0.026mm. The accuracy of the Laser Line Probe when mounted to the Platinum Faro Arm is reduced to 0.061mm.

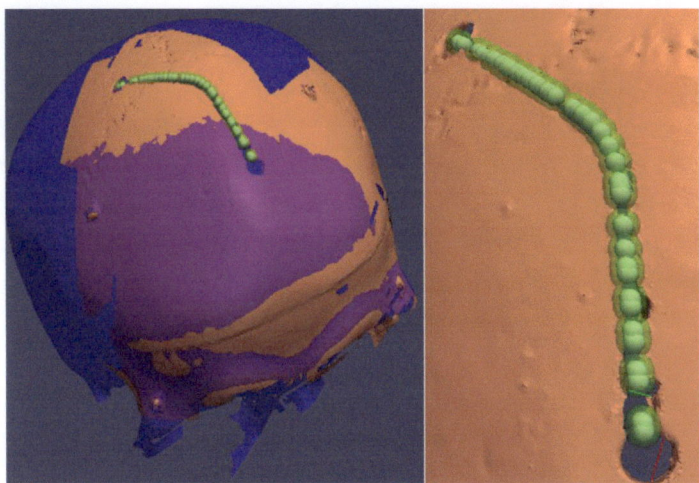

Figure 11.1.: Assessment of trajectory cutting accuracy. Left picture shows registered and overlaid laser scans taken before and after performing the cut with the robot. Right view shows assessment of cut.

Polaris Optical Tracking Camera

The Polaris ©Optical Tracking Camera is from Northern Digitial Inc. and has an accuracy of 0.30mm RMS within the extended Pyramid (which was employed) at distances from 950mm up to 3000mm from the camera. The 95% confidence interval for the repeatability of the measurement is at 0.5mm. The system provided measurements at 30Hz.

11.1.3. Software Used

GeoMagic Qualify

GeoMagic Qualify ©(www.geomagic.com) provided the interface to the FARO Laser Scanner for the point collection. The included package, GeoMagic Wrap, provided the data processing package for point cloud to 3D polygon transformation, mesh repair, and mesh reduction.

Vistrails

VisTrails is an open-source scientific workflow and provenance management system developed at the University of Utah that provides support for data exploration and visualization (www.vistrails.com). The program provides a graphical workflow building concept for interfacing with VTK. It additionally allow custom code to be inserted using Python Scripting, and allows the visualisation and comparison of workflow results, from multiple runs using a graphical spreadsheet interface.

11.1.4. Offline Assessment Results - Simple Geometries

Table 11.1 shows the measured accuracy of the system measured using the workflow in the previous section.

Table 11.1.: Average accuracies achieved by the Craniostar on different trajectories

Surface	Trajectory	±0.5mm	±1mm
Flat Wood	Single straight 5cm segment	97.20%	100.00%
Flat Wood	Single curved 90° segment with 4cm radius	98.15%	100.00%
Flat Wood	Two 5cm segments joined with 45° join	97.60%	100.00%
Plastic Phantom Skull	Single straight 5cm segment	97.00%	100.00%
Plastic Phantom Skull	Single curved 90° segment with 4cm radius	95.00%	100.00%
Plastic Phantom Skull	Two 5cm segments joined with 45° join	95.60%	100.00%

11.1.5. Offline Assessment Results - Complete Procedures

Several complete procedures were performed for a variety of different patient anomalies. Some of these results are shown in Figure 11.2. The result of accuracy assessments for the complete procedures however indicated lower accuracy than that of the simple geometries. The main reason this occurs, is due to a requirement for re-registration in the middle of the procedure. This re-registration occurs when the robot must operate on both sides of the skull. This means that the optical tracking system much be moved as well as the rigid body marker, such that complete coverage can be achieved. The end result is a slight misalignment between the two trajectory halves. This can be seen in Figure 11.3. When the above workflow is used for assessment of the accuracy, large sections of the trajectory can fail to register correctly, and the inaccuracy can be measured with <75% at ± 1mm. For extreme cases, this can be below 60%. When these same procedures are reviewed from the online logging, discussed later in the next section, we can see that the system was tracking, and controlling the robot continually to < 0.5mm for over 95% of the procedure. It therefore appears to be a failure of the optical tracking system implementation, as opposed to the robot design or control system.

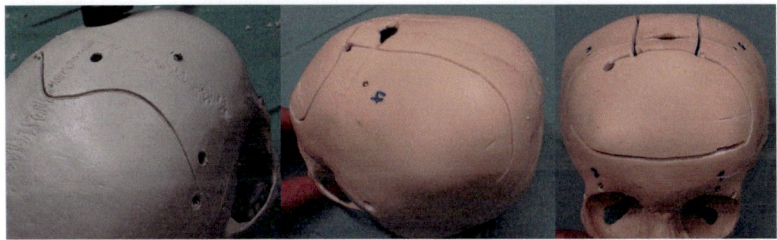

Figure 11.2.: Examples of trial results

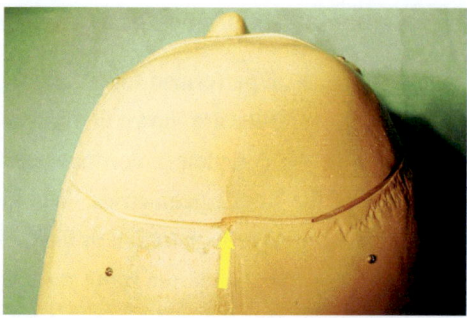

Figure 11.3.: Misallignment of trajectory cuts due to Re-Registration

11.1.6. Online Logging Assessment Results

The online logging by the system tracked the parameters that the system was using to operate. One of these parameters was the lateral offset of the cutting axis from the trajectory. This parameter was first logged to allow a tuning of the control system, but was later seen as an online assessment of accuracy. Example plots of this parameter from simple geometry cuts are shown in Figures 11.4 and 11.5. In both these graphs we can see an initial placement error of the robot, followed by a correction of the trajectory. In the first graph, we can measure a ±0.5mm accuracy of >95%, and in the second >99%. This same concept was repeated for the more complex trajectories; however, the lateral offset was replaced with an assessment of 3D locations that are closest between the trajectory and cutting axes. Figure 11.6 shows a 3D view of this trajectory tracking.

11.1.7. Discussion of Assessment Results

These graphs provided in the last section, were very typical of the results from logging. The graphs here show only the first few centimeters recorded for the trajectory cutting, and if a longer cut was recorded, this limit of this accuracy would approach 100%. The reason for this initial error is the human placement of the robot. While the GUI does allowed placement of

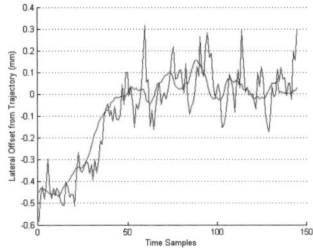

Figure 11.4.: Lateral Error Logged from start of trajectory cut, example 1. Blue is actual recorded values, Red is 10 sample running average.

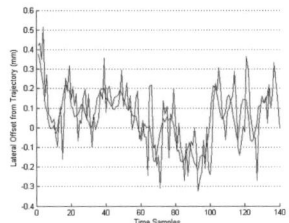

Figure 11.5.: Lateral Error Logged from start of trajectory cut, example 2. Blue is actual recorded values, Red is 10 sample running average.

the robot very accurately, to within this 0.5mm, in practice it was found quite difficult. When the robot is being placed, the spikes on the wheels grip quickly. They also prevent any fine tuning of the placement by sliding of the robot.

It was also commented by the surgeons that this first stage of the trajectory is not of great concern. The hole drilled is already considerably larger than the trajectory to be cut, and if the first few millimeters of the trajectory are only a slight enlargement of the hole, this would be deemed acceptable.

One other problem occurring during the phantom studies was that the plastic of the phantoms was not completely cut, instead a certain percentage of the plastic was only melted and stayed on the underside of the phantom, hindering the progress of the robot. This is shown in Figure 11.7. It is not believed this affected the accuracy of the robot; however, monitoring the torque of the motors of the robot indicated that the robot did have to work considerably harder. This placed more stress on the wheels, and the requirement to maintain friction.

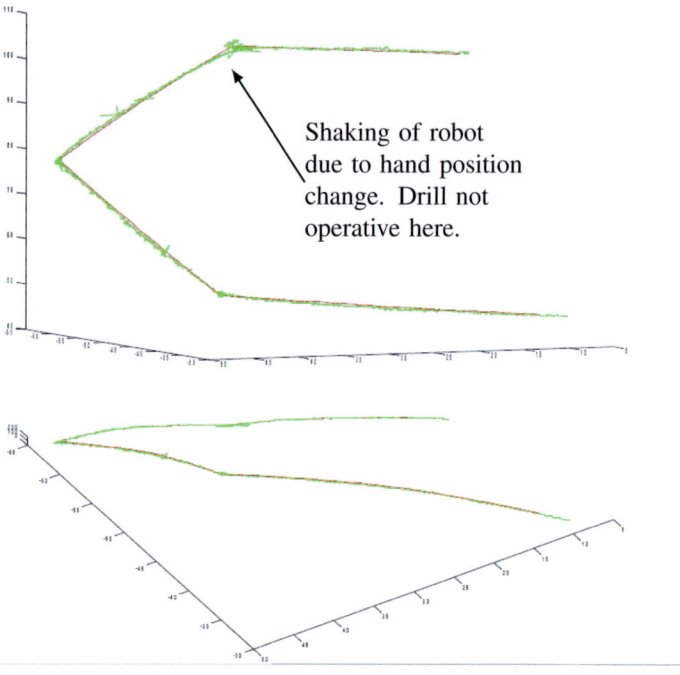

Shaking of robot due to hand position change. Drill not operative here.

Figure 11.6.: 3D Tracking of complex trajectory. Red line is trajectory. Green line is tracked robot. Axis ticks are at 5 and 10mm.

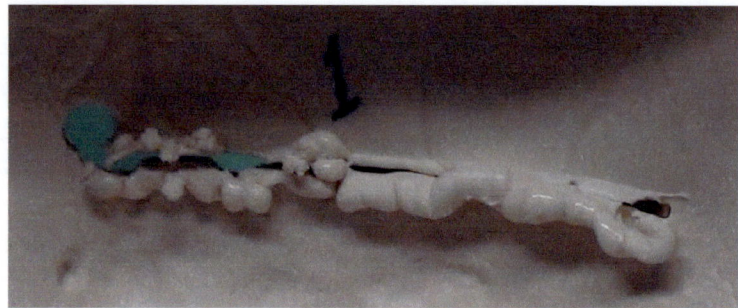

Figure 11.7.: Problem with plastic Phantoms used for Craniotomy Trials. The cut material is not completely removed, but partially melts and hinders future movement.

11.2. Impact Assessment

The complete system was tested in a mock surgery using a Swine Skull as phantom. A Figure of the setup is shown in Figure 11.8. The same procedure as for section 11.1.1 was used; however, the emphasis here was placed on the additional impact to the skull from other issues.

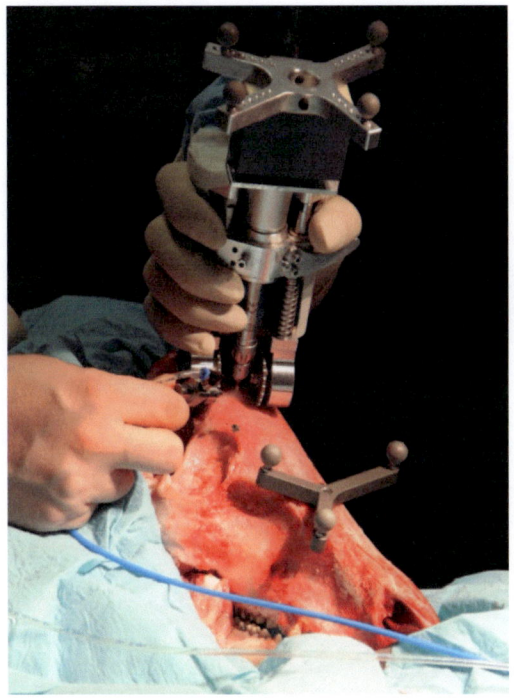

Figure 11.8.: Simulated Surgery Trials for Impact Assessment.

11.2.1. Wheel Damage

In normal use of the Robot, the impact shown in Figure 11.9 was documented. In this example, there is a clear mark left by the traversal of the

159

spiked wheels over the skull. Of note however, is that there was penetration of the spikes identifiable by laser scanning the surface. This indicates that the damage is completely superficial and for a patient acceptable. With further tests however, it was found that the robot could damage the skull if working on a highly curved surface. In Figure 11.10 we can see an example of this damage.

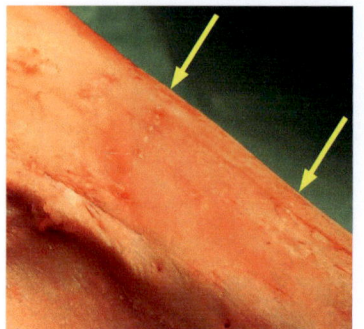
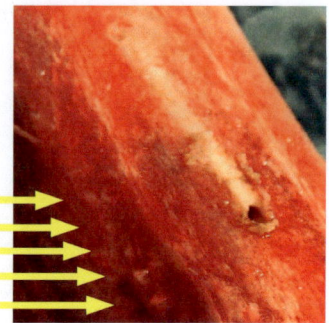

Figure 11.9.: Damage by wheel spikes moving over prepared bone surface. Two wheel tracks are indicated by yellow arrows.

Figure 11.10.: Damage by wheel spikes is increased when angle of wheels to surface is more acute. The wheel spikes' damage are indicated by the yellow arrows.

11.2.2. Cut

After performing a cut with the robot, the bone was photographed and laser scanned. Figure 11.11 shows one of these photos. The resulting cut is smooth.

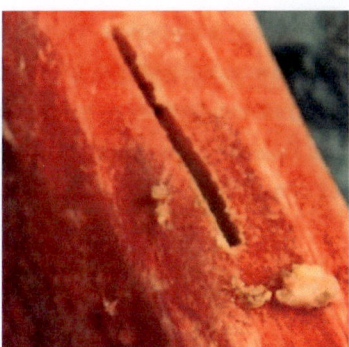

Figure 11.11.: Bone Cut from robot is smooth and consistent.

11.2.3. Discussion of Impact Results

Due to the fact that the Swine Skull is considerably thicker than that of a human patient, it was also not possible to achieve complete penetration of the cut. This meant that the robot could not use the craniotomy hook to achieve a counter force on the counter side of the skull. It was therefore only possible to place extra force on the wheels through the surgeon pushing on the robot. Within the scope of the simulated surgery, there was no possibility to measure the force applied; however, it was noted that during the cut, the craniotomy was not completed inserted into the skull, and video analysis showed that the average penetration was 5mm. Because the surgeon is still holding the top half of the robot, the only force applied comes through the spring system. The 5mm compression indicates this would be approximately equal to that applied during a normal surgery, and the assessment of from the wheel damage is still relevant.

11.3. Conclusions

The system has demonstrated the ability to cut a trajectory within 0.5mm of a planned route; however, this accuracy is unfortunately not able to be maintained over a complete trajectory. There are a number of errors noted that prevent this accuracy being maintained. For example, the initial start location of the robot by the surgeon can mean the first few millimeters of the trajectory are slightly outside the 0.5mm before the control system has time to recover. Because these first few millimeters are inside of connected with a bore hole that is considerably larger than the width of th trajectory to be cut, the impact of such an error is deemed very low.

More significant was the error in re-registration of the patient during a trajectory. This was required when the complex trajectory requires the robot to be completely on both sides of the skull, and a repositioning of the optical tracking system is required. The result is a misaligned registration leads to a greater error in assessment of this accuracy. This problem could also be alleviated with further integration of a multiple camera tracking system, or a complete Operating Room optical tracking system.

12. Conclusion

Conclusion

In this thesis an intuitive system for robotic assisted surgery is introduced. The combination of a navigation system and a wheeled hand-held robot form an integral solution for surgical craniotomies that bring minimum impact into the Operating Room. The complete system was developed, inclusive of the mechatronic design of the robot, the communications architecture, the software GUI, algorithms for control and additional safety systems that ensured the system would be safe to proceed towards clinical trials.

Special attention was focused throughout this system development on the interaction of the robotic system with the surgeon. Here it was seen as key to involve the surgeon in the control, and not remove them from the procedure.

The mechatronic design of the robot, was extended past the prototype used for testing to include a complete 4 axis control including depth cutting and angle cutting. The robot was engineered to be capable of handling autoclaving sterilisation. This was achievable by a disconnectable motor module, with self-aligning connectors.

The control system developed was modified from previous works by Keo et al. for application on a non-linear 3D surface. This required redefinition of the Frenet formulation to avoid negative effects on the control parameters from the under actuated degrees of freedom of the robot, such as tilt and lean. This control system was made highly intuitive for the surgeon, with use of these under actuated degrees of freedom. The tilt was used as one of the inputs for the robot, such that a simple push / pull control could be achieved. This was also combined with the foot pedal for the craniotomy drill, such that no external controls were required for the system. Activation of the Craniotomy Drill also activated the control for the robot. This activation was also used for resetting the coordinate space of the robot, such that the push-pull control could be used with the robot starting in any possible orientation.

The testing was completed on a number of different surfaces and phantoms. The system demonstrated the ability to consistently cut simple trajectories to < 0.5mm. This accuracy was slightly lost on larger more complex trajectories when multiple registrations were required to gain optical tracking coverage over the entire skull surface. It was also pointed out that this would not be a problem with optical tracking systems using multiple cameras or fused tracking systems. With examination of the data logging, it was seen that despite the registration errors, the system was cutting to within 0.5mm of the planned trajectory over the complete skull. Additionally examined during the testing was the impact of the complete system on the entire operating room procedure. Here analysed was the workflow impact, and additional points such as the smoothness of the cut, and damage due to the spiked wheels of the system.

Finally, the system demonstrated the ability to cross the gap between completely capable but large and obstructive robotic systems, and the 'steady hand assistant' category of intelligent tools, and in conclusion the presented methods significantly contribute to increasing the acceptability of medical robots by surgeons. The interaction between surgeon and robot becomes more intuitive and friendlier. The complete system control with auxillary features such as power and safety components is capable of being built into one box 30 cm x 30 cm x 10 cm. This is seen as being highly acceptable for integration into the Operating Room. Moreover, the additional safety features developed and implemented can be used for a variety of other systems, without requiring a large degree of integration.

Future Prospects

While many ideas were scoped out and presented in the Design Concepts chapter, the wheeled robot was seen as showing the most potential for this design. However it should also be noted that the other ideas were presented here in detail because they were all seen as feasible systems, and may be developed in the future. The wheeled robot, as well as these systems may find additional applications for other surgical operations such as knee or implant sculpting, but additionally they may also prove beneficial outside of the medical area in industrial robotics as well. For example, both the wheeled robot and creeping robot could be used for the cutting of sheet metal. The Swinging Robot could be employed in a variety of tasks, not only in this small varient, but at a larger level, ceiling mounted for example holding a variety of tools. Finally there still remains the possibility to push this robot further into clinical trials. The system is proven, and with further integration of complete Operating Room optical tracking, the system could see even better results and accuracies. Additionally the one mechatronic element that remains to be optimised is the spike shape for the wheels.

A. Standard Workflow

The following appendix covers the 18 steps that form a typical craniosyn-ostosis procedure. Clearly due to the abnormality of this illness, there is rarely a completely standard procedure.

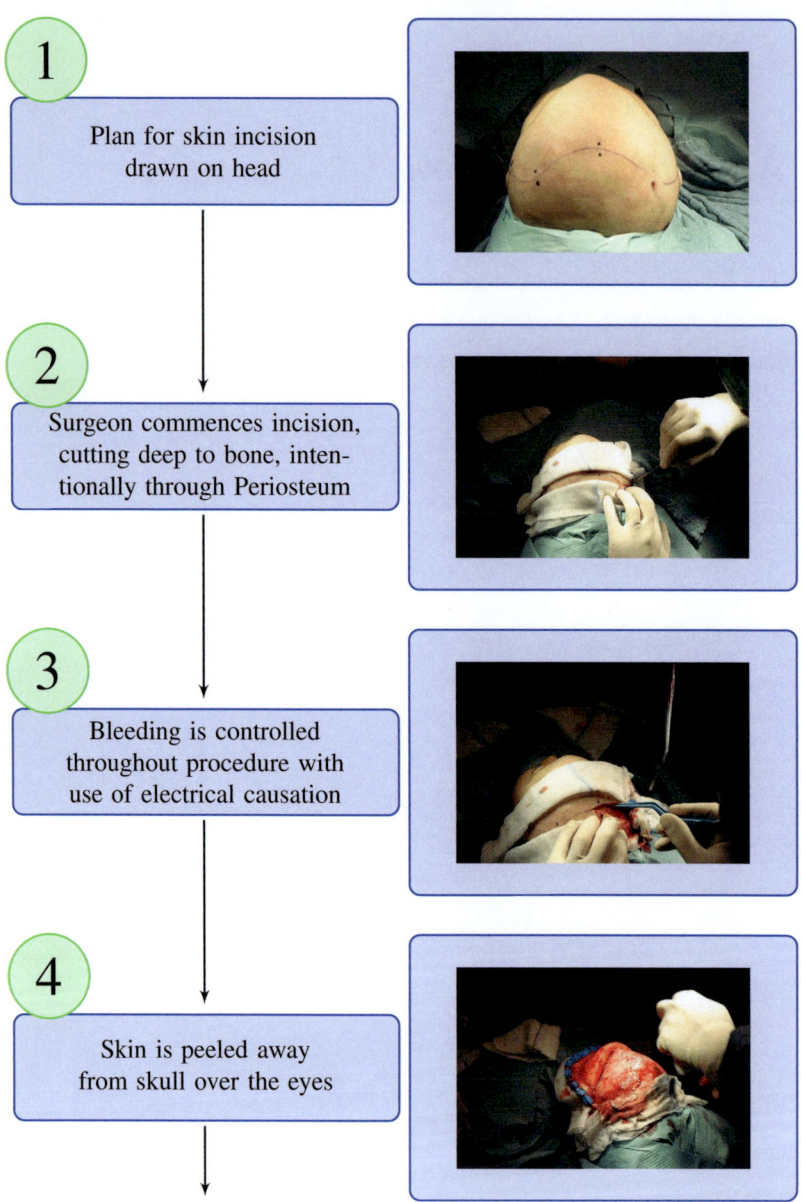

1 Plan for skin incision drawn on head

2 Surgeon commences incision, cutting deep to bone, intentionally through Periosteum

3 Bleeding is controlled throughout procedure with use of electrical causation

4 Skin is peeled away from skull over the eyes

Figure A.1.: Steps 1 through 4 of the craniotomy

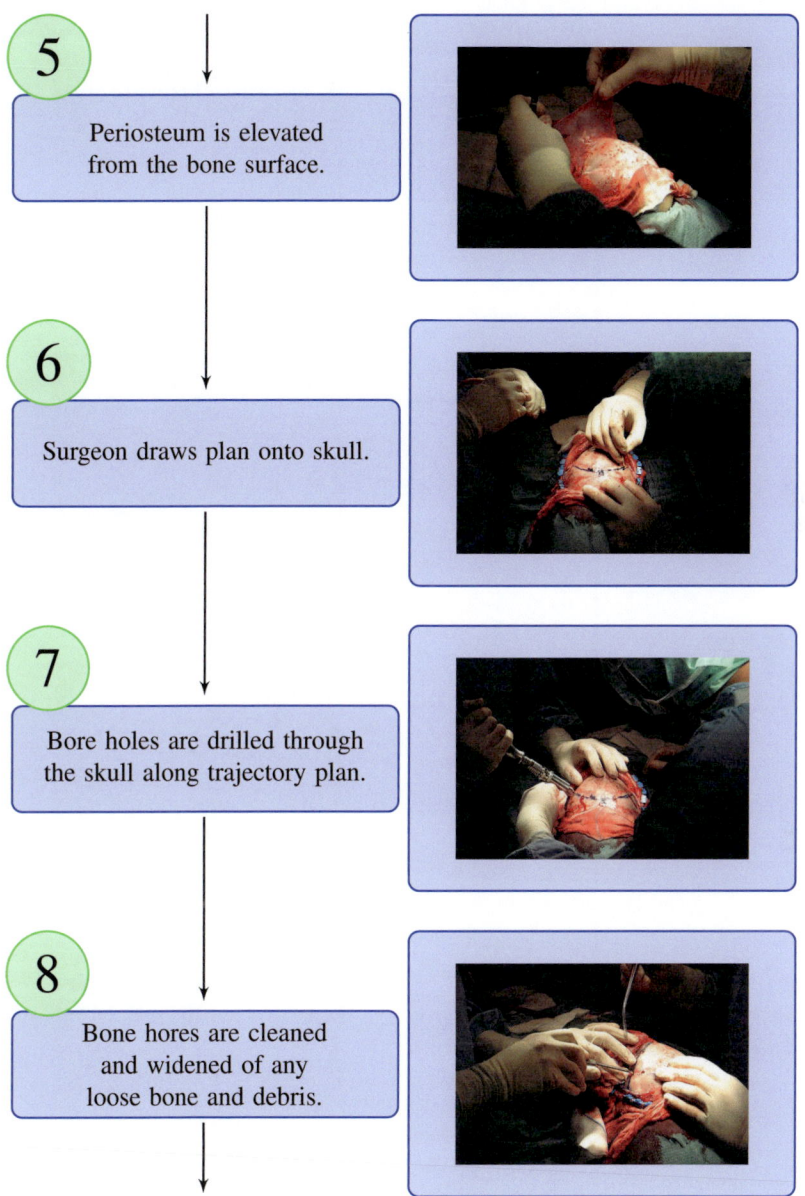

5 — Periosteum is elevated from the bone surface.

6 — Surgeon draws plan onto skull.

7 — Bore holes are drilled through the skull along trajectory plan.

8 — Bone hores are cleaned and widened of any loose bone and debris.

169

Figure A.2.: Steps 5 through 8 of the craniotomy

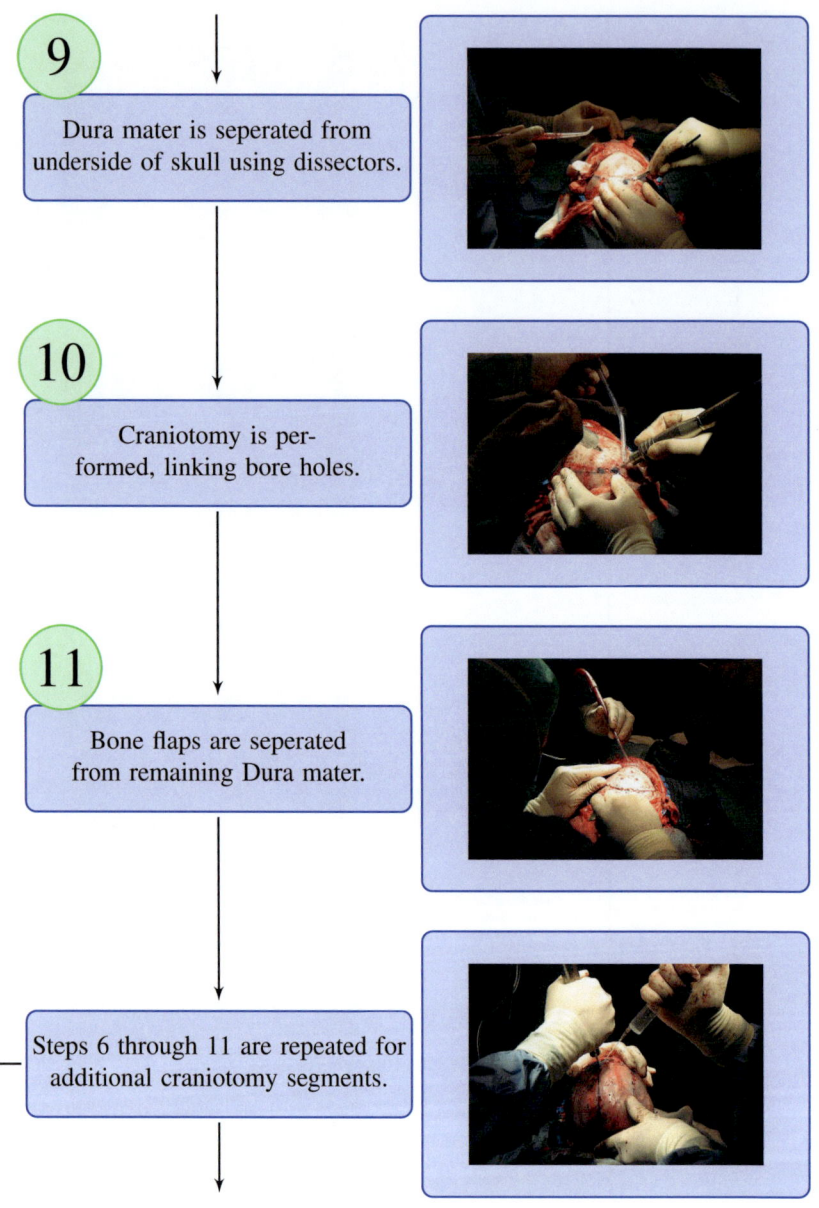

9 Dura mater is seperated from underside of skull using dissectors.

10 Craniotomy is performed, linking bore holes.

11 Bone flaps are seperated from remaining Dura mater.

Steps 6 through 11 are repeated for additional craniotomy segments.

Figure A.3.: Steps 9 through 11 of the craniotomy

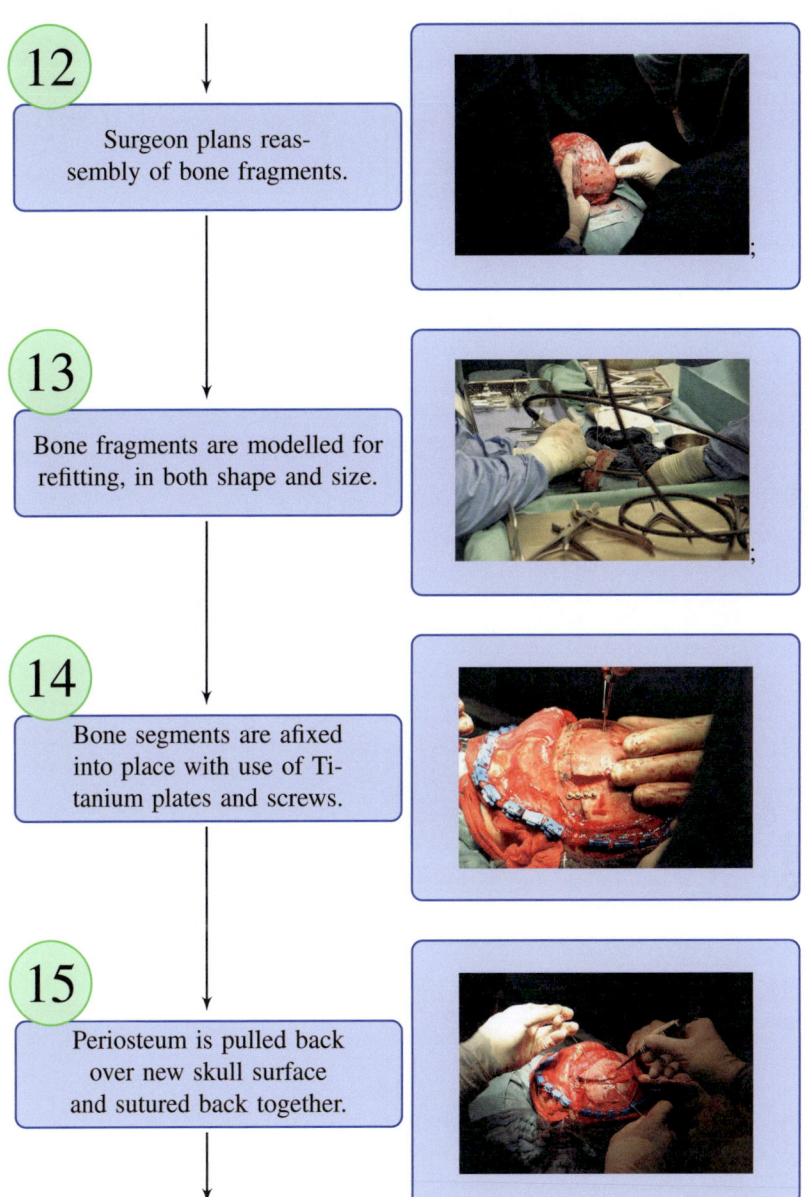

12 Surgeon plans reassembly of bone fragments.

13 Bone fragments are modelled for refitting, in both shape and size.

14 Bone segments are afixed into place with use of Titanium plates and screws.

15 Periosteum is pulled back over new skull surface and sutured back together.

Figure A.4.: Steps 12 through 15 of the craniotomy

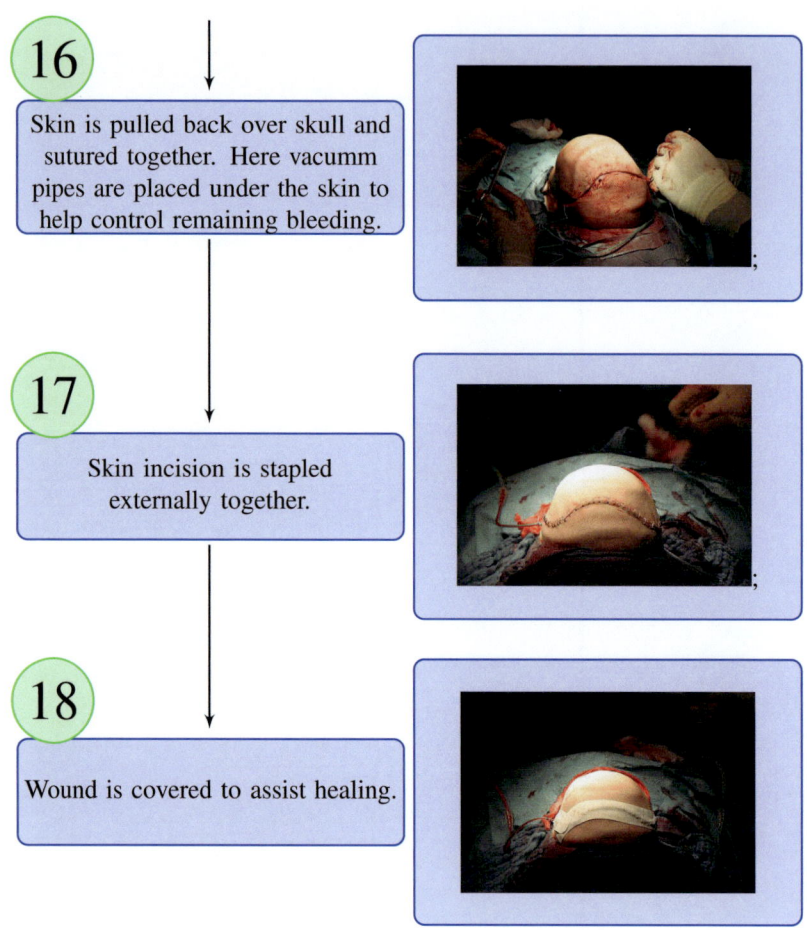

16 Skin is pulled back over skull and sutured together. Here vacumm pipes are placed under the skin to help control remaining bleeding.

17 Skin incision is stapled externally together.

18 Wound is covered to assist healing.

Figure A.5.: Steps 16 through 18 of the craniotomy

List of Figures

List of Tables

Bibliography

[1] Din en iso 17665-1:2006 - sterilization of health care products – moist heat – part 1: Requirements for the development, validation and routine control of a sterilization process for medical devices.

[2] Fachinformation: "das prinzip der dampfsterilisation". Technical report, Gesellschaft für Zentralsterilisation von Medizinprodukten, 2009.

[3] J. Allum, V. Dietz, and H. Freund. Neuronal mechanism underlying physiological tremor. *J Neurophysiol*, 41:557–571, 1978.

[4] D. Altobelli, R. Kikinis, J. Mulliken, H. Cline, W. Lorensen, and F. Jolesz. Computer-assisted three-dimensional planning in craniofacial surgery. *Plast Reconstr Surg*, 92:576–585, 1993.

[5] Y. Barzilay, M. Liebergall, A. Fridlander, and N. Knoller. Miniature robotic guidance for spine surgery - introduction of a novel system and analysis of challenges encountered during the clinical development phase at two spine centres. *The International Journal of Medical Robotics and Computer Assisted Surgery*, 2, 2006.

[6] P. Bast, M. Engelhardt, W. Lauer, K. Schrmeder, V. Rohde, and K. Radermacher. Identification of milling parameters for manual cutting of bicortical bone structures. *Computer Aided Surgery*, 8:257–263, 2003.

[7] P. Bast, A. Popovic, T. Wu, S. Heger, M. Engelhardt, W. Lauer, K. Radermacher, and K. Schmeider. Robot- and computer-assisted

craniotomy: resection planning, implant modelling and robot safety. *Int J Med Robotics Comput Assist Surg*, 2:168–178, 2006.

[8] G. Bellus, K. Gaudenz, E. Zackai, L. Clarke, J. Szabo, and C. Francomano. Identical mutations in three different fibroblast growth factor receptor genes in autosomal dominant craniosynostosis syndromes. *Nat Genet*, 14:174–176, 1996.

[9] E. M. Boctor, R. J. W. III, H. Mathieu, A. M. Okamura, and G. Fichtinger. Virtual remote center of motion control for needle-placement robots. *Computer Aided Surgery*, 9(5/6):1–9, 2004.

[10] E. S. Boy, E. Burdet, C. L. Teo, and J. E. Colgate. Motion guidance experiments with scooter cobot. In *Proc. 11th Symposium on Haptic Interfaces for Virtual Environment and Teleoperator Systems HAPTICS 2003*, pages 63–69, Mar. 22–23, 2003.

[11] E. S. Boy, E. Burdet, C. L. Teo, and J. E. Colgate. Investigation of motion guidance with scooter cobot and collaborative learning. *IEEE Transactions on Robotics*, 23(2):245–255, Apr. 2007.

[12] G. Brisson, T. Kanade, A. DiGioia, and B. Jaramaz. Precision free-hand sculpting of bone. *MICCAI 2004, LNCS 3217*, pages 105–112, 2004.

[13] R. Bucholz, W. Macneil, P. Fewings, A. Ravindra, L. McDurmont, and C. Baumann. Automated rejection of contaminated surface measurements for improved surface registration in image guided neurosurgery. *Stud Health Technol Inform*, 70:39–45, 2000.

[14] Burgmueller. *Drawing of a Child at Birth, Age 1, Age 2*. Countway Library, Boston, 1723.

[15] J. Burgner, M. Mueller, J. Raczkowsky, and H. Woern. Robot assisted laser bone processing: Marking and cutting experiments. In

Advanced Robotics, 2009. ICAR 2009. International Conference on, 22-26 June 2009.

[16] J. C.A. Moore, M. Peshkin, and J. Colgate. Cobot implementation of virtual paths and 3d virtual surfaces. *IEEE Transactions on Robotics and Automation*, 19(2):347–351, Apr. 2003.

[17] B. Carlisle. Robot mechanisms. In *Proc. IEEE Int. Conf. on Robotics and Automation, San Francisco, CA,, pp 701-708*, 2000.

[18] S. Chanphat and W. Wannasuphoprasit. A novel transformable cobot. In *Proc. IEEE Conference on Robotics, Automation and Mechatronics*, pages 1–6, Dec. 2006.

[19] W. Chop, B. Green, and A. Levi. Fluoroscopic guided targeting system with a robotic arm for pedicle screw insertion. *Neurosurgery*, 47(872-878), 2000.

[20] M. Cohen. Editorial: perspectives on craniosynostosis. *J Med Genet*, 136:313–326, 2005.

[21] A. Collignon, D. Vandermeulen, P. Suetens, and G. Marchal. Surface based registration of 3d medical images. *Proceedings of SPIE*, 5749:32–42, 1993.

[22] S. Crouzet, G. Haber, W. White, K. Kamoi, A. Berger, R. Goel, I. Gill, and J. Kaouk. Single-port, single-surgeon robotic assisted in reconstructive urology. *The Journal of Urology*, 181(4 (Supplement)):552, 2009.

[23] J. Currey. The effects of strain rate, reconstruction and mineral content on some mechanical properties of bone. *J. Biomechanics*, 8:81–86, 1975.

[24] B. Davies. A review of robotics in surgery. *P I Mech Eng H*, 214:129–139, 2000.

[25] F. D. del Rio, G. Jimenez, J. Sevillano, C. Amaya, and A. C. Balcells. A new method for tracking memorized paths: Application to unicycle robots. *Proceedings of the 10th Mediterranean Conference on Control and Automation - MED2002 Lisbon, Portugal*, 2002.

[26] Y. Dong, L. Zhang, D. Lu, R. Bernbardt, and D. Surdilovic. A novel cobot and control. In *Proc. Fifth World Congress on Intelligent Control and Automation WCICA 2004*, volume 5, pages 4635–4639, June 15–19, 2004.

[27] G. Dudek and M. Jenkin. *Computational Principles of Mobile Robotics*. Cambridge University Press, 2000.

[28] G. Eggers, J. Klein, J. Blank, and S. Hassfeld. Piezosurgery an ultrasound device for cutting bone and its use and limitations in maxillofacial surgery. *British Journal of Oral and Maxillofacial Surgery*, 42:451–453, 2004.

[29] G. Eggers and J. Muehling. Template-based registration for image-guided skull base surgery. *Otolaryngology Head and Neck Surgery*, in submission(Georgs article of Jaw Splint Registration in Maxillo Facial Area), 2007.

[30] G. Eggers, H. Senoo, G. Kane, and J. Muehling. The accuracy of image guided surgery based on cone beam computer tomography image data. *Oral Surgery, Oral Medicine, Oral Pathology, Oral Radiology, and Endodontology*, Volume 107, Issue 3:Pages e41–e48, March 2009.

[31] B. Eldridge, K. Gruben, D. LaRose, J. Funda, S. Gomory, J. Karidis, G. McVicker, R. Taylor, and J. Anderson. A remote center of motion robotic arm for computer assisted surgery. *Robotica*, 14(01):103–109, 1996.

[32] D. Engel, J. Raczkowsky, and H. Woern. Robacka: Ein robotersystem fuer den einsatz in der chirurgie. *Rechner- und sensorgestuetzte Chirurgie, Proceedings zum Workshop*, 4:279 – 286, 2001.

[33] F. Evans. Stress and strain in bones. *Springfield, Charles C. Thomas*, Il1, 1957.

[34] R. Faulconbridge. *Systems Engineering - Body of Knowledge, Revised Edition*. Magpie, Applied Technology, Kingston ACT, Australia, 2001.

[35] E. Faulring, J. Colgate, and M. Peshkin. A high performance 6-dof haptic cobot. In *Proc. IEEE International Conference on Robotics and Automation ICRA '04*, volume 2, pages 1980–1985, Apr. 2004.

[36] J. Fearon, D. Singh, S. Beals, and J. Yu. The diagnosis and treatment of single-sutural synostoses: are computed tomographic scans necessary? *Plast Reconstr Surg*, 120:1327–31, 2007.

[37] A. Feicke, M. Baumgartner, S. Talimi, D. Schmid, H. Seifert, M. Maentener, M. Fatzer, T. Sulser, and R. Strebel. Robotic-assisted laparoscopic extended pelvic lymph node dissection for prostate cancer: Surgical technique and experience with the first 99 cases. *European Urology*, 55:876–884, 2009.

[38] J. Fitzpatrick, R. Balachandran, and R. Labadie. Bite-block relocation error in image-guided otologic surgery. *MICCAI 2004*, LNCS 3217:518–525, 2004.

[39] J. Fitzpatrick, J. West, and C. Maurer. Predicting error in rigid body registration. *IEEE Trans Med Imaging*, 17(5):694–702, 1998.

[40] A. Follman, J. Little, K. Schraeder, A. Forff, M. Engelhardt, and K. Radermacher. Synergistic control - semiautomatiche navigation eines neuartigen trepanationsinstrumentes. *Proceedings CURAC 08*, pages 111–112, 2008.

[41] R. B. Gillespie, J. E. Colgate, and M. Peshkin. A general framework for cobot control. In *Proc. IEEE International Conference on Robotics and Automation*, volume 3, pages 1824–1830, May 10–15, 1999.

[42] P. Gleason, R. Kikinis, D. Altobelli, W. Wells, E. A. 3rd, P. Black, and F. Jolesz. Video registration virtual reality for nonlinkage stereotactic surgery. *Stereotact Funct Neurosurg*, 63:139–143, 1994.

[43] A. Gleizal, J. Bera, B. Lavandier, and J. Beziat. Piezoelectric osteotomy a new technique for bone surgery - advantages in craniofacial surgery. *Childs Nerv Syst*, 23:509–513, 2007.

[44] M. Gomez-Blanco, C. N. Riviere, and P. K. Khosla. Sensing hand tremor in a virtreoretinal microsurgical instrument. *tech. report CMU-RI-TR-99-39*, Robotics Institute, Carnegie Mellon University, December, 1999.

[45] H. Gordon. Craniostenosis. *J Br Med*, 2:792–795, 1959.

[46] G. Grevers, A. Leunig, A. Klemens, and H. Hagedorn. Cas of the paranasal sinuses - technology and clinical experience with the vector-vision-compact-system in 102 patients. *Laryngorhinootologie*, 81(476-483), 2002.

[47] W. Grimson, G. Ettinger, S. White, P. Gleason, T. Lozano-Perez, W. W. 3rd, and R. Kikinis. Evaluating and validating an automated registration system for enhanced reality visualization in surgery. *In: Ayache N, ed: Proceedings of CVRMed 95. Lecture Notes in Computer Science*, 905:3–12, 1995.

[48] W. Grimson, G. Ettinger, S. White, T. Lozano-Perez, W. W. 3rd, and R. Kikinis. An automatic registration method for frameless stereotaxy, image guided surgery, and enhanced reality visualization. *IEEE Trans Med Imaging*, 15:129–140, 1996.

[49] S. Hansson. Surface roughness parameters as predictors of anchorage strength in bone: a critical analysis. *Journal of Biomechanics*, 33:1297–1303, 2000.

[50] R. C. Harwell and R. Ferguson. Physiologic tremor and microsurgery. *Microsurgery*, 4:187–192, 1983.

[51] S. Hassfeld and J. Muehling. Computer assisted oral and maxillofacial surgery, a review and an assessment of technology. *Int. J. Oral Maxillofac. Surg*, 30:2–13, 2001.

[52] J. Henderson, K. Smith, and R. Bucholz. An accurate and ergonomic method of registration for image-guided neurosurgery. *Comput Med Imaging Graph*, 18:273–277, 1994.

[53] M. Howard, M. Dobbs, T. Simonson, W. LaVelle, and M. Granner. A noninvasive, reattachable skull fiducial marker system. *J Neurosurg*, 83(Banana Splint 1995):372–376, 1995.

[54] M. Huang, W. Mouradian, S. Cohen, and J. Gruss. The differential diagnosis of abnormal head shapes: separating craniosynostosis from positional deformities and normal variants. *Cleft Palate-Craniofac J*, 35:204–11, 1998.

[55] B. Hutchison, A. Stewart, and E. Mitchell. Characteristics, head shape measurements and developmental delay in 287 consecutive infants attending a plagiocephaly clinic. *Journal Compilation Foundation Acta Paediatrica*, Vol. 98, Issue 9:1494 – 1499, 2009.

[56] H. Kabbani and T. Raghuveer. Craniosynostosis. *Am Fam Phys*, 69:2863–70, 2004.

[57] G. Kane, G. Eggers, R. Boesecke, J. Raczkowsky, H. Wörn, R. Marmulla, and J. Mühling. Intuitively controlled handheld mobile robot for precision craniotomy surgery. *Poster to 13th International*

Conference on Human-Computer Interaction, San Diego, USA, IN PRINT, 2009.

[58] G. Kane, G. Eggers, R. Boesecke, J. Raczkowsky, H. Wörn, R. Marmulla, and J. Mühling. System design of a hand-held mobile robot for craniotomy. *MICCAI*, 2009.

[59] G. Kane, G. Eggers, H. Ionescu, V. Vieira, R. Boesecke, J. Raczkowsky, H. Wörn, and R. Marmulla. Feasibility and medical impact assessment of handheld-mobile-robot usage in image guided craniotomy. In O. Doessel and W. C. Schlegel, editors, *World Congress on Medical Physics and Biomedical Engineering*, volume 25. Springer, September 2009. Munich, Germany.

[60] T. Keaveny, E. Morgan, and O. Yeh. Standard handbook of biomedical engineering and design. pages 8.1–8.24, 2004.

[61] P. Kelly, B. Kall, and S. Goerss. Results of computed tomography-based computerassisted stereotactic resection of metastatic intracranial tumors. *Neurosurgery*, 22:7–17, 1988.

[62] H. K. Khalil. *Nonlinear Systems, 2nd edn*. Prentice Hall, Englewood Cliffs, NJ, 1996.

[63] B. Kim and P. Tsiotras. Controllers for unicycle-type wheeled robots: Theoretical results and experimental validation. *IEEE Transactions on Robotics and Automation*, 18(3):294–307, 2002.

[64] P. Knappe, I. Gross, S. Pieck, J. Wahrburg, S. Kuenzler, and F. Kerschbaumer. Position control of a surgical robot by a navigation system. *International Conference on Intelligent Robots and Systems (IROS)*, Vol 4, Issue 27-31:3350–3354, 2003.

[65] W. Korb, R. Marmulla, J. Raczkowsky, J. Mühling, and S. Hassfeld. Robots in the operating theatre chances and challenges. *Int. J. Oral Maxillofac. Surg*, 33:721–732, 2004.

[66] G. Laborde, J. Gilsbach, A. Harders, L. Klimek, R. Moesges, and W. Krybus. Computer assisted localizer for planning of surgery and intra-operative orientation. *Acta Neurochir (Wien)*, 119:166–170, 1992.

[67] E. Lajeunie, M. L. Merrer, C. Bonaiti-Pellie, D. Marchac, and D. Renier. Genetic study of nonsyndromic coronal craniosynostosis. *American Journal of Medical Genetics*, 55:500–504, 1985.

[68] E. Lajeunie, M. L. Merrer, D. Marchac, and D. Renier. Syndromal and nonsyndromal primary trigonocephaly: Analysis of a series of 237 patients. *American Journal of Medical Genetics*, 75:211–215, 1998.

[69] S. Lavallee, P. Sautot, J. Troccaz, P. Cinquin, and P. Merloz. Computerassisted spine surgery: a technique for accurate transpedicular screw fixation using ct data and a 3-d optical localizer. *J Image Guid Surg*, 1:65–73, 1995.

[70] J. Lee, C. Lin, C. Huang, S. Lee, and C. Wu. A navigation system for brain surgery using computer vision technology. *Lecture Notes in Computer Science*, 5128:289–299, 2008.

[71] B. Long, B. Rebsamen, E. Burdet, and C. Teo. Development of an elastic path controller. In *Proc. IEEE International Conference on Robotics and Automation ICRA 2006*, pages 493–498, May 15–19, 2006.

[72] B. Long, B. Rebsamen, E. Burdet, H. Yu, and C. Teo. Elastic path controller for assistive devices. In *Proc. 27th Annual International Conference of the Engineering in Medicine and Biology Society IEEE-EMBS 2005*, pages 6239–6242, Jan. 17–18, 2006.

[73] K. H. Low and Y. P. Leow. Kinematic modeling, mobility analysis and design of wheeled mobile robots. *Advanced Robotics*, 19:73–99, 2005.

[74] D. Lu, L. Zhang, L. Wang, and J. Shen. Architecture and trajectory constraint control of a five bar cobot. In *Proc. Fifth World Congress on Intelligent Control and Automation WCICA 2004*, volume 6, pages 4960–4963, June 15–19, 2004.

[75] D. Marchac and D. Renier. *Craniofacial surgery for craniosynostosis*. Little Brown, Boston, 1982.

[76] R. Marmulla. Computer aided bone segment navigation. *Habilitationsschriften der Zahn-, Mund-und Kieferheilkunde*, 2000. Another Test.

[77] R. Marmulla, S. Hassfeld, and J. Mühling. Referenzierung der patientenlage mittels 3d-weichteillaserscan. *Biomedizinische Technik/Biomedical Engineering*, 47:29–32, 2002.

[78] R. Marmulla, J. Muehling, and G. Eggers. Image-to-patient registration by natural anatomical surfaces of the head. *Central European Journal of Medicine*, 2(1):89–102, 2007.

[79] J. Matjaz, S. Harris, F. Baena, P. Gomes, and B. Davies. The acrobot system for total knee replacement. *Industrial Robot: An International Journal*, 30(1):61–66, 2003.

[80] C. Maurer and J. Fitzpatrick. Review of medical image registration. *In: Maciunas RJ, ed: Interactive Image-Guided Neurosurgery. Park Ridge, IL: American Association of Neurological Surgeons*, pages 17–44, 1993.

[81] P. McKerrow. *Introduction to Robotics*. Addison Wesley, 1991.

[82] M. Mehrwald, J. Burgner, C. Platzek, C. Feldmann, J. Raczkowsky, and H. Wörn. Analysis of the short-pulsed co2 laser ablation process for optimising the processing performance for cutting bony tissue. *SPIE*, 2010.

[83] A. Meystel. *Autonomous Mobile Robots - Vehicles with Cognitive Control*. World Scientific, Singapore, 1991.

[84] C. A. Moore, M. A. Peshkin, and J. E. Colgate. Design of a 3r cobot using continuous variable transmissions. In *Proc. IEEE International Conference on Robotics and Automation*, volume 4, pages 3249–3254, May 10–15, 1999.

[85] C. A. Moore, M. A. Peshkin, and J. E. Colgate. Cobot implementation of 3d virtual surfaces. In *Proc. IEEE International Conference on Robotics and Automation ICRA '02*, volume 3, pages 3242–3247, May 11–15, 2002.

[86] J. Mühling, J. Reuther, and N. Sörensen. Prämature schadelnahtsynsotsen. *Neue Wege der Chirurgischen Behandlung Klinikarzt*, 16:724, 1987.

[87] A. Nabavi, G. Manthei, U. Blomer, L. Kumpf, H. Klinge, and H. Mehdorn. Neuronavigation. computer-assisted surgery in neurosurgery. *Radiologe*, 35:573–577, 1995.

[88] C. Nathan, V. Chakradeo, K. Malhotra, H. D'Agostino, and R. Patwardhan. The voice-controlled robotic assist scope holder aesop for the endoscopic approach to the sella. *Skull Base*, 16(3):123–131, 2006.

[89] N. Nathoo, M. Cavusoglu, and M. Vogelbaum. In touch with robotics: neurosurgery for the future. *Neurosurgery*, 56:421–433, 2005.

[90] O. Olivo, G. Maj., and E. Toajari. Sul significato della minuta struttura del tessuto osseo compatto. *Boll. Sc. Med. Bologna*, 109:369–394, 1937.

[91] A. Ollero, A. Garcia-Cerezo, and J. Martinez. Fuzzy supervisory path tracking of mobile reports. *Control Engineering Practice*, 2, Issue 2:313–319, 1994.

[92] B. H. P. Dario and A. Menciassi. Smart surgical tools and augmenting devices. *IEEE Trans. Robot. Automat.*, 19(5):782–792, 2003.

[93] P. Pan, K. Lynch, M. Peshkin, and J. Colgate. Human interaction with passive assistive robots. In *Proc. 9th International Conference on Rehabilitation Robotics ICORR 2005*, pages 264–268, June 28–July 1, 2005.

[94] H. Paul, W. Bargar, B. Mittlestadt, P. Kazanzides, B. Musits, J. Zuhars, P. Cain, B. Williamson, and F. Smith. Robotic execution of a surgical plan. *IEEE International Conference on Systems, Man and Cybernetics*, 2:1621 – 1623, 1992.

[95] M. A. Peshkin, J. E. Colgate, W. Wannasuphoprasit, C. A. Moore, R. B. Gillespie, and P. Akella. Cobot architecture. *IEEE Transactions on Robotics and Automation*, 17(4):377–390, Aug. 2001.

[96] P. Pott, A. Käpfle, A. Wagner, E. Badreddin, R. Männer, P. Weiser, H. Scharf, and M. Schwarz. Erste versuche mit dem handgehaltenen operationsroboter itd. *In: Boenick U (Hrsg.) Bolz A (Hrsg.): Biomedizinische Technik Beiträge zur 38. Jahrestagung der Dt. Gesellschaft für biomediznische Technik im VDE Bd. 49*, Fachverlag Schicle & Schän GmbH:72–3, 2004.

[97] A. Raabe, R. Krishnan, R. Wolff, E. Hermann, M. Zimmermann, and V. Seifert. Laser surface scanning for patient registration in intracranial image-guided surgery. *Neurosurgery*, 50:797–801, 2002.

[98] A. Raabe, R. Krishnan, R. Wolff, E. Hermann, W. Zimmermann, and V. Seifert. Laser surface scanning for patient registration in intracranial image-guided surgery. *Journal of Neurosurgery*, 50(4):797–803, 2002.

[99] M. Reichmann. *Ein Modell zur Entwicklung neuartiger chirurgischer Eingriffe am Beispiel der Minimal Traumatischen chirurgie*. PhD thesis, Department of Informatics, 2010.

[100] C. N. Riviere and P. S. Jensen. A study of instrument motion in retinal microsurgery. *Proceedings of the 22nd International Conference of the IEEE Engineering in Medicine and Biology Society*, Chicago, July 23-28,, 2000.

[101] C. Samson. Path following and time-varying feedback stabilization of a wheeled mobile robot. *Proc. Int. Conf. ICARCV92, Singapore*, RO13.1, 1992.

[102] C. Samson and K. Ait-Abderrahim. Feedback stabilization of a nonholonomic wheeled mobile robot. *IEEE Proceedings IROS 1991*, pages 1242–1247, 1991.

[103] J. Schlaier, J. Warnat, and A. Brawanski. Registration accuracy and practicability of laser-directed surface matching. *Journal of Computer Aided Surgery*, 7(5):284–90, 2002.

[104] O. Schneider and J. Troccaz. A six-degree-of-freedom passive arm with dynamic constraints (padyc) for cardiac surgery application: Preliminary experiments. *Comp Aid Surg*, 6:340–351, 2001.

[105] O. Schorr, J. Moenchenberg, and J. R. und H. Woern. Kasop - a generic system for pre- and intraoperative surgical assistance and guidance. *Proceedings of the 15th International Congress and Exhibition of Computer Assisted Radiology and Surgery (CARS)*, 2001.

[106] A. Schramm, N. Gellrich, and R. Gutwald. Indications for computer-assisted treatment of cranio-maxillofacial tumors. *Comp Aid Surg*, 5(Gold Plated solution is Fiducial Markers):343–352, 2000.

[107] K. Seo and J. Lee. Kinematic path-following control of a mobile robot under bounded angular velocity error. *Advanced Robotics*, 20(1):1–23, 2005.

[108] D. Shin. *High performance tracking of explicit paths by roadworthy mobile robots*. PhD thesis, Carnegie Mellon, 1990.

[109] R. Sibson. Studies in the robustness of multidimensional scaling: Perturbational analysis of classical scaling. *J. Roy. Statist. Soc.*, 41:217–229, 1979.

[110] H. Stanton and H. Mersmann. Swine in cardiovascular research. *CRC Press, Inc.*, 1 and 2, 1986.

[111] S. Stenirri, G. Restagno, G. B. Ferrero, G. Alaimo, L. Sbaiz, C. Mari, L. Genitori, F. Maurizio, and L. Cremonesi. Integrated strategy for fast and automated molecular characterization of genes involved in craniosynostosis. *Clinical Chemistry*, 53 10:1767–1774, 2007.

[112] P. Stevens, L. Hollier, and S. Stal. Post-operative use of remoulding orthoses following cranial vault remodelling: a case series. *Prosthet Orthot Int*, 31:327–41, 2007.

[113] D. Stoianovici and R. Taylor. Medical robotic systems in computer-integrated surgery. *Probl. Gen. Surg.*, 20:1–9, 2003.

[114] A. Straulino, S. Daeuber, G. Eggers, J. Raczkowsky, S. Hassfeld, and H. Wörn. Generating normative data of the cranium using spherical harmonics. 1268:1306, 2004.

[115] D. Surdilovic and H. Simon. Singularity avoidance and control of new cobotic systems with differential cvt. In *Proc. IEEE International Conference on Robotics and Automation ICRA '04*, volume 1, pages 715–720, 2004.

[116] J. Sutcliffe and J. J. Wright. *The Sculptor and Art Student's Guide to the Proportions of the Human Form With Measurements in Feet and Inches of Full Grown Figures of Both Sexes and Various Ages The Plates Reproduced by John Sutcliffe From the Original Treatise entitled Polycletus by Dr. Gottfried Schadow The Text Translated from the German by James J. Wright.* 1883.

[117] M. Swindle, A. Smith, and B. Hepburn. Swine as models in experimental surgery. *J Invest Surg*, 1:65–79, 1988.

[118] T. Takizawa. Isocentric stereotactic three-dimensional digitizer for neurosurgery. *Stereotact Funct Neurosurg*, 60:175–193, 1993.

[119] R. Taylor. A perspective on medical robotics. *Proceedings of the IEEE*, 94(9):1652–1664, 2006.

[120] R. Taylor, H. Paul, P. Kazandzides, B. Mittelstadt, W. Hanson, J. Zuhars, B. Williamson, B. Musits, E. Glassman, and W. Bargar. An image-directed robotic system for precise orthopaedic surgery. *IEEE Trans. Robot. Automat.*, 10(3):261–275, 1994.

[121] R. H. Taylor. A model-based optimal planning and execution system with active sensing and passive manipulation for augmentation of human precision in computer-integrated surgery. *Proceedings of the Second International Conference on Experimental Robotics, Toulouse, France*, 1991.

[122] R. H. Taylor. *Medical robotics*. Computer and Robotic Assisted Knee and Hip Surgery. Oxford Univ. Press, Oxford, U.K., 2004.

[123] R. H. Taylor, R. Kumar, and P. Jensen. Experiments with a steady hand robot in constrained compliant motion and path following. *Proceedings of the 1999 IEEE International Workshop on Robot and Human Interaction*, pages 92 – 97, 1999.

[124] S. Ueno, Y. Imai, T. Hayasaka, M. Okubo, T. Ishikawa, and T. Yamaguchi. Development of a mobile toilet system servicing elderly on call. *IFMBE Proceedings*, 22, Part 11:1747–1749, 2009.

[125] W. Wannasuphoprasit, R. Gillespie, J. Colgate, and M. P. M.A. Cobot control. *International Conference on Robotics and Automation*, 1997.

[126] S. Weihe, C. Schiller, C. Rasche, S. Hassfeld, M. Wehmaeller, H. Knoop, M. Epple, and H. Eufinger. Cad-cam prefabricated individual skull implants: new aspects in robot resection and guided bone regeneration. *International Congress Series*, 1268:584–590, 2004.

[127] J. West and C. M. R. M. J.M. Fitzpatrick, S.A. Toms. Fiducial point placement and the accuracy of point-based, rigid body registration. *Neurosurgery*, 48(4):810–817, 2001.

[128] T. Worsnopp, M. Peshkin, J. E. Colgate, and K. Lynch. Controlling the apparent inertia of passive human-interactive robots. In *Proc. IEEE International Conference on Robotics and Automation ICRA '04*, volume 2, pages 1179–1184, Apr. 2004.

[129] L. Yin, S. Venkatesan, S. Kalyanasundaram, and Q. Qin. Effect of microstructure on micromechanical performance of dry cortical bone tissues *Materials Characterisation*, 60:1424–1431, 2009.

[130] J. Zöller, A. Kübler, W. Lorber, and J. Mühling. *Kraniofaziale Chirurgie: Diagnostik und Therapie kraniofazialer Fehlbildungen*. Thieme, 2003.